Invested to be Molested
WHY YOU SHOULD FIRE YOUR FINANCIAL ADVISOR NOW!

Other Titles
Gold Wars: the Battle for the Global Economy
A Spiritual Autopsy of Science and Religion

Fiction
Wildcard
Song of Solomon
Scar Jones
Tara Born of Tears (May, 2015)

CONTENTS

Why you should Read this Book

Psychopaths make up 10% of the financial services industry - 10 X the national average ~ Canadian forensic psychologist Robert Hare from Washington's Blog.

Your life savings is in serious danger. The threats are numerous. As detailed in this book, if you are not careful, if you do not take charge or your own financial situation, you will steadily lose money in real terms and possibly be wiped out.

The chairman of Forbes Media, in an interview, said 3 frightening things about investment realities:

1. Federal Reserve methods are causing damage to older people - and it's intentional.

2. Financial Advisers are taking nearly 70% of client returns.

3. The boomer generation will not make it through retirement - many will go broke.

Forbes laid out a 'permanent flaw' built right into the financial structure, and it punishes investors. Your Financial Adviser (or FA throughout the book) probably has most of your money in mutual funds. The Flaw requires such fund directors to hold more than 75% flat equities - instruments that will underperform. Most investors are losing tens, even hundreds of thousands of dollars even as you read this. People are retiring much older - and some not at all. It's created a slow-motion disaster in the private investor market. That flaw is an important part of this book. But it's just the tip of the iceberg. The financial services industry is designed to rob you with your blessing by keeping you ignorant. And unfortunately, it's very, very good at what it does.

In a survey, a quarter of finance pros claimed unethical action is essential to succeed in the industry. And 1 out of 3 claimed the regulatory and pay structure pushed people to behave unethically and even illegally. Analysts find these numbers to be low because of self-reporting - advisors do not want to draw attention to their own actions through a survey, so they naturally lie to cover up. Most of these analysts find the numbers low based on personal conversations with friends in the industry. Fraud is rampant and systemic. It is the way things are done.

I was working on the oil rig in 2008 when I found out some pretty nasty stuff about our political system that made me start investigating. I'd been a 'buy-and-hold' investor in mutual funds off and on for 15 years, but this got me digging deeper. The system was (and still is) seriously out of whack and tilting to the side. I began telling people that something big was going to happen with the economy. I got lucky with the timing, to be sure, but the crash happened a few months later. When I warned them, my friends thought I was going a little nuts. Afterwards, nobody mentioned that I was right! It was pretty disheartening and I felt more than a little isolated. But it began a multi-year journey toward understanding the global economy and the many factors that make it so uncertain these days. The primary factor that rose to the top was manipulation.

When I wrote Gold Wars: the Battle for the Global Economy I was quite entrenched. I had nothing to lose, nothing to protect, and nothing to push. I had no agenda but to tell people what was really going on - and it was bad.

You (or someone you know) have your life savings at risk - serious risk - from the Financial Services Industry. It's in a variety of ways - conflicts of interest, rehypothecation, collateralization, limited book, restricted offerings, churning, ditching the 'bad' book on clients, limits on protective setups, analysts time restrictions, the 'secret' tax, dangers of a currency collapse, the derivatives black hole, the debt crisis, disinformation and on and on. Financial Services is extraordinarily complex - probably needlessly so - and the pitfalls and traps are almost unlimited. The days of buy and hold are long gone - a 2008 style crash is almost inevitable again. Only this time, the government may be unable to bail the system out. And believe me, when it happens, Wall Street will profit from your losses. They are ready and you are prey. That's why Goldman Sachs analysts refer to clients as 'muppets.'

This most venerable firm on Wall Street short sold its clients bad bonds, which then crashed by 50%. GS then bought the bonds back at profit. It was illegal, unethical, and a really bad idea for maintaining clients - but they didn't suffer any ill consequences. No investigation, no prosecution, no SEC snoops looking around. No matter how much they stuck it to their own clients illegally, they walked away counting their (stolen) money. And GS staffers have routinely become heads of the US Treasury, SEC lead staff, Central Bank heads of England, and even unelected President of Italy! It's a powerful company and it's creating the new financial system.

You are being deceived by a systematic 'redaction.' All the economics studies in conventional schooling forbids a whole range of issues. Any teacher talking about them will soon find himself censured or out on the pavement. Corrupted and manipulated capital markets, bankrupt financial orgs, monetary stimulus as a destroyer of wealth, bail-ins (using private bank accounts to rescue troubled banks), huge decline in percent of people in labor force, bizarre stock values, corrupted accounting legalized, fraudulent government statistics, $26 trillion bailout from 2008-9, the failure of QE, the loss of low-risk investments (CD's pay less than 1%?!?), secret machinations to twist the markets (Exchange Stabilization Fund), the control by big banks over the Fed, the control of the Pentagon by weapons manufacturers, unrepayable debt - public, corporate, and private, the perversion of mass media by centralized ownership - feeding you dangerous nonsense, and the theft of government accounts like Social Security to keep the game going. Just the thin end of the wedge of what's being withheld from your kids in their college classes - and from your trusty financial adviser.

There is an excess of knowledge in this book - more than you need. But it has been carefully chosen to be helpful. It is all useful at some level. Some people will use certain aspects, others will different aspects. Later, you may find that such knowledge is extremely beneficial and it will be necessary - at least to explain what's happening in a seemingly chaotic world. It's a chess term called 'overprotection,' or in military terms 'dry powder.' During the blunderbuss days, if your powder got wet, you were useless. You needed dry powder to go into battle, and each soldier carried his own gunpowder. Dry powder here is cash reserves ready to move. If you have none, when opportunity knocks, you can't do anything with it.

However this book advises against keeping large amounts of cash in general. The best approach is to keep 10-15% in a very stable, dividend paying investment. It's a standard practice. Mostly, in standard practice, 90% of your investments will be there. I don't consider this an investment, it's a place to store reserves while awaiting opportunity. There is a very sound reason for staying away from currency, especially the main one.

The US dollar is in the process of repudiation. The world will no longer tolerate the debt excesses and other forceful means of maintaining the dollar's world reserve status. Currently, Russia, China and their allied nations are forging currency swaps (which create trade in those currencies), trade negotiations, and creating alternate means of payments - outside the US dollar. The BRICS central bank is an official project and will soon become a real central bank. When the majority of global trade is no longer conducted in the US dollar - those nations holding US debt will unload it. Then the system will go off the rails. The Fed and major banks currently have a system of interest rate swaps to artificially increase demand for Treasuries. That system will not maintain itself coherently in the face of a mass global sell-off. It is already so unbalanced that such a wrecking ball will turn it into financial chaos. You do not want to be on the wrong side of this trade.

While the government can and will cover all redemptions with more printing, they cannot force the entire world to accept paper it no longer wants in exchange for real goods. Oil will no longer be for sale primarily in dollars. Things will become much more expensive in the US. The dollar will also be worth a lot less domestically and abroad.

I don't give this issue a moral weight, but whether right or wrong, one thing is clear: the dollar / Treasury complex is dying. It won't be gone anytime soon, but it will die as the world's primary reserve currency. This is the critical seismic event that savvy investors are positioning themselves for. If you fail to recognize it, you will be wiped out. And I would bet anything that your advisor has never even mentioned such a possibility. If you brought it up, he probably expressed some concerns about long-term dollar strength, but waved away any serious concerns about a precipitous drop in value. He might have referred to 'doom and gloom.' However, the day will arrive. After a steep rise, the dollar will have a sudden fall. The potential triggers are too numerous to mention, but the prepared investor has this pending occurrence at the top of his list. He knows it is coming.

The Dirty Secret from a Nobel Prize Winner about your Financial Advisor

Daniel Kahneman examined a team of elite financial advisors. As the winner of the Nobel Memorial Prize for economics, Kahneman's studies carry some serious weight. He found these super-elite money managers were no good. Some years some advisors did well, other years other advisors. None of them beat the market over time. In a multi-year tracking, none was better than any other. The correlation to any particular advisor besting another was exactly z-e-r-o. There is no skill to these advisors. And quite importantly - these were the best. These advisors would not even speak to you or me - we don't have the money. They manage money for people with hundreds of millions. And they SUCK.

The managers he gave this news to were dead surprised. They thought they had the mojo. They thought they were the best. He showed them there was no best. What did they do? They bought him a nice dinner and said goodbye. They threw this valuable data, which could really be used to help their clients, into the round file. It quickly disappeared down the memory hole and these same advisors probably still honestly believe they are better than the market, better than the rest.

Now one caveat: as shown throughout this book, the system is not client friendly. It is meant to take money from Main Street to Wall Street. As such, these advisors hands were somewhat tied by existing regulations and protocols. Their companies made a ton of money, at client expense. It is possible (though I doubt it) that the advisors could have done much better if they had put client interests first rather than their own pocketbooks. But then they would be out of a job for not making money for the company. The hidden reality is ugly - advisor and firm interests are aligned against the client. Sad to say, but it is true and this book brings the evidence.

The lack of skill is attributable, in part, to poor choices. Kahneman also did this in a particular company. It is plausible that the company had a particular set of assumptions that all advisors operated on or were forced to align to a particular stream of investments. They were fed the company line. However, that is true of almost any company, and definitely all the big names. It is true on a secondary level of the entire industry. The industry is forced to operate on a specific bias which rewards the companies for keeping their clients in specific investments and punishes them for putting clients in other investments - especially gold and silver. Of course, this punishes clients by denying them the best opportunities. Again and again, this can be shown.

Yet investors ignore it. This study was the strongest proof that different advisors have more skill than others (at least within the systemic restraints). It was done by a Nobel economist. Yet it was politely ignored. The financial services industry did not follow up on it. Why? Because it shows they are dangerous to clients. No further proof is needed - the industry is not acting in client interests. It is actively betraying the client. This is apparent to anyone who can add 2 + 2.

If they were acting in client interests, they would, at the very least, dig into this study. They would make an issue of it, and express some serious concern. It would be a headline topic at industry conferences. But it vanished. To publicize this study in any way would be to damn themselves - and there is no integrity or will in the industry. Who would put their money into an industry that does nothing for them? Who would line up to be the smiling dupe of a predatory industry?

The way out of this trap is to work outside the parameters - outside the constraints of the financial services industry. Do not put your money in their paradigm. And you can beat the market and do well, in fact. Do not diversify a la modern portfolio theory, do not invest in mutual funds, do not buy fee-loaded instruments, etc. These basic advisor investments are all loaded against you.

These experts do use high-level skills. They can evaluate balance sheets, income statements, management quality, cash flow, market share and competition in their analyses. It does mandate very strong training and a high skill set, no doubt about that. But it ignores the fundamental question - are these factors already baked into the stock price? Or are they not there?

No trader can answer this question in a fundamental way. In fact, the question is easily answered for large and mid-cap, heavily researched companies. 'Yes' - these factors are included because the big money has done so much research and there is such heavy trading that the price point inclusive of these factors is quickly found by the market.

It's a reason why small cap can be a better investment for overall returns, but it can be worse because the market may not factor in negative information. The truth is traders do not know of their own blind spot here. They are unaware of it and virtually all of them so.

In another study, Philip Tetlock pulled 80,000 predictions from political experts with a simple question for a variety of political situations. 'Will there be more [of a certain situation - like war, liberty, etc] less, or the same amount of it?] The experts performed worse than a random answer. They were wrong more than 67% of the time. A baby would have done better picking out numbered chits for answers. Expertise and intuition interfered with valid predictions. Even in areas where they were considered the best, experts did no better, and often worse, than randomly chosen persons. The experts may not be at fault, they may be taking into account too much information, making it difficult to understand all the possibilities.

The upshot? No advisor - political or financial - has a clue. Your FA will talk a good game - that's his training, but he will do worse than random guessing. Even the highest paid advisors fail the most basic test - they cannot beat the market.

It is basically set up to transfer money slowly from Main Street to Wall Street. There is some evidence that this transfer is picking up speed, too, in a variety of ways. One is the inflationary trend, where money comes from the FED spigot, rather than Main Street directly. But the middle class loses value in their savings. They lose absolute money, but not nominal money - they never perceive the loss. A different transfer is the sudden loss of large sums, a la 2008. Many people with high-paid advisors took a serious gut-punch in '08. But your advisor got paid the same while you ate mud. Still with him? You might rethink that.

Most investors with advisors are investing against their own interests - they don't to do the research to understand it well. Fortune magazines most admired companies showed that the worst rated companies (rated by financial advisors) earned MUCH higher returns over a 20 year period. They vote against the winners. The firms least admired for profitability and value significantly outperformed, in investor returns, those that were most admired - the ones you were recommended. In a sense, that's a great nutshell for investing. It's also a key investing metric - the stock market is largely illusory. But when we hear something, a few bits and pieces come together. Sometimes this coherence seems very compelling. Getting excited and irrational, investors - all of us - make mistakes. That's because poor evidence can make a great story.

Kahneman calls this the 'illusion of validity.' This illusion keys into one of his most important studies: it's the illusion of stock-picking skill. One of the things found in this study - highly active traders do not do well. Slower moving traders have better returns. (This is old information, predating high-frequency trading. HFT traders often do very well flipping in and out of trades thousands of times a minute, using computer algorithms.)

But it brings out another fascinating finding. Since men are more prone to act on hunches, women tend to perform better as traders. Women are far more cautious in trading and that caution pays off by not making quick choices. I learned this the hard way and have lost my share of money in the market. (Just an aside - anybody who claims they have never lost money in the markets is either a liar or has never been in the market. Their advice is dangerous.)

Kahneman also found the mutual fund problem. These funds are operated by some fairly sophisticated, long-term financial professionals. Having been in the game 25 years at least, these managers do know their markets well. The funds are run by large teams because it's a large sum of money. Even so, 7 of 10 mutual funds underperform the baseline market. Mutual funds are a losing bet. And they are far and away the most likely place your fund manager will put you. Often, he hasn't been certified to put you in better investments. He's not allowed to. And you take the hit.

Regulators

Insider understand one unbreakable rule: they don't criticize other insiders ~ Larry Summers, former secretary of the Treasury, to Elizabeth Warren

Most of the exchanges in Canada have recently become for-profit entities. The Toronto Stock Exchange, most notably. There used to be six exchanges, but now there are only three. The TMX operates most of the exchanges. The ICP- who oversees futures and commodities - is no longer a non-profit organization. The Investment Industry Regulatory Organization of Canada (IIROC) is still a non-profit, but it is a non-governmental organization. It is heavily lobbied and more or less controlled by members in the organization. When added to the mix that these industries and organizations are 'self-regulating' (not regulated by laws), you have a recipe for wide-scale fleecing of investors. Obviously, they want to maintain the image of integrity even if there is no integrity there. So nobody gets totally robbed - everybody just gets continually milked.

How the end-game scenario plays out is unclear, but it not favorable for the average investor. These are companies with intricate knowledge of the way markets move and extremely sophisticated software. Often the brokers function as market makers and have an opposing position to their own clients - an easily identified conflict of interest. That knowledge can be used to decimate market sectors after short-selling through unassociated organizations and other unsavory tactics. All they need do is deny any connection and withhold data. The regulators are toothless because they are owned by the regulated companies.

In the Canadian Securities exam study guide, there is about a page devoted to ethics. 'Ethical trading is critical to the functioning of capital markets, since without assurances regarding the behavior of market participants it would be hard to attract investors.' So ethics is basically a functional situation having nothing to do with right and wrong, legal or illegal, or the morality of property rights and theft. The bottom line - if it scares away investors, then it's unethical. But if you can fleece investors and still keep money flowing in - well, that's ethical. There is no ethical breach. So if investors do not know what's going on (if it's theft), then it's ethical.

'Unethical conduct includes any omission, conduct or manner of doing business which in the opinion of the disciplinary body is neither in the public interest nor the interest of the exchange.' (my italics). Note the clever use of words. If the behavior is in neither interest, it is unethical. However, if the business is in the interest of the exchange, but not the public interest, it satisfies the definition of being ethical. They can self-servingly rip off investors, all day long and that's ethical.

In the US, the situation is the same only different, as they say. The original SEC was (humorously enough) the Securities Exchange Company, run by (wait for it) ...Charles Ponzi. Ponzi, of course, was the inventor of the Ponzi scheme whereby early investors profit from later investors with no valid means of capital growth. Bernie Madoff ran a Ponzi scheme.

The modern iteration of the SEC is the Securities and Exchange Commission. The SEC is notorious for its pronounced laxity. From the mortgage crisis, there have been no prosecutions despite a littered trail of evidence. Falling down on the job, asleep at the switch, paid for revolving door, ineffectual, toothless regulatory agency - take your pick. That's what happens when an industry is 'self-regulating' through an 'independent' government agency. The execs at various companies get top-level jobs in the SEC itself and protect their friends in the father-land from the pitchforks and jail bars. As a wronged investor, you will receive nothing but the illusion of assistance from the SEC. The phenomenon even has a name - regulatory capture - when large corporate cartels get their own people in place in the overseeing agencies. The public has no real means of protection.

And if you want more proof that the regulators are owned by the regulated, then look no further than HSBC. One of the 5 largest banks in the US, HSBC was proven, in court and in Congress to be laundering drug money. The 2012 proceedings showed, beyond any doubt, that the entire corps of senior execs was in on the drill. They knew that $700 billion in drug money was funneled through a series of maze-like accounts, profiting the bank the whole way, of course. HSBC was fined less than 1/10th of a percent of its profits on this scheme. No one was indicted, the bank was not given criminal charges. The fine was just a cost of business, and not much of one at that. In fact, Lord Green was the UK chair of the bank during the period of malfeasance. Now he is the finance minister for the country.

Naturally, they have a great reason. Attorney General Eric Holder said,

I am concerned that the size of some of these institutions becomes so large that it does become difficult for us to prosecute them when we are hit with indications that if you do prosecute, if you do bring a criminal charge, it will have a negative impact on the national economy, perhaps even the world economy.

These too big to fails are also Too Big to Prosecute. Why? They are called G-SIFI's, meaning Globally Systemically Important Financial Institutions. If one fails, they all get dragged down by the 'derivative web.' That's a $1000 TRILLION (over a quadrillion dollars) net of parlays, bets, and interest rate swaps - the Elmer's binding the paper mache global (ahem - Western) economy together. Holder is right - if one fails, the whole charade implodes. There's too much interconnectivity and too, too, too much debt. And guess what? If they decide to stick it to you (look in the rearview - already happened and happened again), do you think the regulators are going to do anything?

The new Financial Stability Board lists 28 banks in this category. This board is comprised entirely of former executives from the banks themselves. The FSB has stated, categorically, with an official backing of the United States Department of Justice, that the largest financial institutions in the world are ABOVE the LAW.

Since someone in the banks committed the crimes, those people are also above the law. They can make money however they want - no criminal activity is restricted - and they will not go to jail. They will not be prosecuted. There will be no investigation. Who do you think is protecting your assets? Because it's not the people who have that job.

The fox owns the henhouse.

Financial Advisor Scam

No one has ever seen anything like this . . . if you look at the details of what these central banks are doing, it's all very experimental. . . . There is something fundamentally wrong ~William White, former chief economist of the Bank for International Settlements

Multiple Conflicts of Interest

To understand the Financial Services system, it is critical to realize the following very significant conflicts of interest and ways they 'sell you out.' For now, here's the short-list - we'll dig into these throughout this book.
- They have limited options
- They make money off of your money - money you lose.
- They are selling their book

- They can lose their license for selling unapproved instruments - like gold.
- They peddle insurance.
- They spend most of their time looking for new clients, not serving existing ones.
- They short sell your stocks.
- They recommend investments that the corporate office is trying to dump.
- They perform no better than index funds on average - worse after fees.
- Your well-being is not their priority - their profit is.
- It is illegal for them to recommend investments outside their license authority.
- They are limited to mutual funds, most often - the absolute dog of all investments. Mutual funds are the cellar where the dumb money gets dumped.
- They won't tell you the stock market is lethal for small investors.

Most firms have quotas, prizes, and bonus payouts for top sellers. No firms offer these incentives for client account performance. Often advisers must bring in $6 million per year or more in new funds to manage. This is energy spent attracting more money for 'da firm' that could (should?) be spent analyzing markets and boosting client performance. On top, they must churn out several hundred thousand in fees - collected from clients. Failure to do so may cause punitive measures - payout percentages cut up to 50%! This is a putsch to cause low earning analysts to quit.

These methods all work against client interests. They do not put you in the ideal investments - ever. Since the primary compensation for your FA is fees from mutual funds (for some its insurance lines), they have no incentive to provide you with their advertised service - financial planning.

The director of financial services firm Synchron said, "licensees are trying to get advisers to sign agreements which impose onerous conditions and financial penalties on exiting advisers and their new licensees in order to make it very difficult for them to leave." Large corporate licensing companies are the worst violators. These companies will not let their contractors out of poor contracts. This is not to retain them per se, but to prevent them going into private practice for themselves. The culture is created that way - this prevents individuals from offering the best advice to their clients. It prevents a fee-based model of advisement. That would be GOOD for the client.

Most financial advisors are decent enough people in their own way. Sure, they have a built-in conflict that they need to put your money at risk. But that's the industry's fault, not theirs. Most of the instruments they put you in are palatable. They will offer a small return over the years. It won't beat inflation, but you will increase your nominal net worth. You will lose spending power gradually as the real value of money is eroded, but most people can't be bothered to understand this problem.

Being a thinking person, you understand the need to beat inflation. Otherwise you're flying backwards. You also understand the need to have access to all the market offers. Why accept restrictions that only benefit your investment company? If your advisor knows of a very good buy - low risk/high yield - he will not put you in it unless his company allows him to. And trust me, he probably can't. The certifications are very restrictive. Most FAs can only use mutual funds - the dog's behind of financial markets. Nobody ever beat inflation in mutual funds. Sure, their literature makes it sound great. But they spin the truth to sell you something you wouldn't really want if you had the time to dig into it.

You don't want to be limited to the selection of 'opportunities' your financial advisor has access to. The industry is structured so that as much money as possible flows into the corporate coffers. Remember, even the most elite financial advisors fail to outperform the market. Some definitely do well on occasion. But when their track record was examined by a world-renowned statistician, they did no better than the Dow Jones over multiple years. And worse - they charge ongoing fees the stock indexes do not. The Dow Jones, by the way, did pretty poorly in the years under study.

Nomi Prins was a senior exec on Wall Street. She became disgusted with the system and walked out on her venerable firm (initials G and S), blowing the whistle on them for customer abuses. The whistle was ignored by regulators who seem to have a habit of letting this company in particular off the hook. Probably because the head of the Fed and Treasury have both been former employees of the company on several occasions. Prins has a blog detailing the many people she helps with the financial predators. Here is a letter she received and posted.

1. You are a conservative saver, and you have a large amount of money in the bank. Since you are a "valued customer", the bank gives you your own personal financial representative, with whom you build a relationship over time. But this person is not on your side. He will prod, coax, and sweet-talk you into moving your savings over to the bank's investment arm.

2. If you do move your money over to the investment bank, your financial advisor will charge you high management fees (upwards of 1% of assets per year). Moreover, you will pay big commissions on top of that. But these won't be disclosed as commissions – they will be incentives disguised in various ways that are buried deep within the fine print. Since you don't know about these, and

since you trust the paid professional you've hired, you will be an easy victim.

3. Because of these incentives, your advisor will dump investments into your portfolio that may include: funds of funds (which charge layers upon layers of fees), IPO offerings that the bank can't manage to sell off, complex structured products, variable annuities, and the like. Anything the bank wants to get rid of, wishes to hawk, or gets a kickback to sell will be dumped into your account. All the while, your advisor will be assuring you that these are excellent investments.

4. The result will be that you will almost certainly do worse than the market overall – at the very least, by the fees and commissions you pay (commissions that have been taken – stolen! – without your consent), and at worst, by scorching losses obtained via inappropriate investments.

5. If you figure out what has happened (and most people don't, they will think that the market just did badly), you will have little recourse. The bank will have forced you to sign a mandatory binding arbitration agreement that shuts you out of the court system. Even if the bank has committed fraud, forgery, etc., it doesn't matter. The courts are closed to you.

6. If you manage to obtain a settlement or get a judgment from the arbitration forum, the results will almost certainly be kept confidential. Therefore, the goings-on are kept quiet, and the banks can continue their practices unabated.

The victims of this fraud are not doing anything wrong or unreasonable. They are working with large national banks. They are hiring certified financial planners. They are paying high management fees, so there is no expectation of anything "free". They are asking good questions and being reassured that their financial advisor is looking out for their best interest. But they are being swindled nonetheless – because they don't know about the hidden incentives, because they are unable to differentiate good investments from bad ones, and because they are being reassured by their advisor about how well they are doing compared to the market, even if the opposite is really true.

These are professional con men that are swindling millions of seniors, every day, all over the country -- decimating their life savings in their final years.

I know, because I have seen it happen.

The sad fact is, these are the biggest banks in the world. They are not some regional bank flying under the radar. In fact, the regional banks are the ones you should work with - they tend to be honest.

For example, Bank of Montreal's Nesbitt Burns club is called the 'President's Council' for most successful advisors. It honors those who bring in the most commissions. Client investment performance is not considered for this club. This stuns even me. Shouldn't client service at least be given a lip service for the giant bank's most prestigious honor?

A commission based financial adviser should get paid only if he makes your money grow. That is his job. If he loses you money, he should not be paid. It's that simple. And it would be easy to do - all he would need do is take a percentage of profits. That should be the industry standard, yet you will never find a single money manager who takes compensation in this way. Why not? They would all starve! Or at least not get rich draining your money. Most make money by essentially taking yours and giving you less in return than you could easily make yourself. Those are the stats I will show in this book. The industry is fleecing the average investor in a multitude of ways.

Here's another story (all too many of these types). The man in question is not being 'robbed.' He's just losing money with his advisor. He'd be better off in cash.

My father is not happy with his financial advisor. He's been working with said advisor since 2005 or so. The advisor is with Wells Fargo - initially Wachovia securities. This individual handles my father's retirement accounts, his practices pension funds for him, and his employees, as well as my family's accounts - specifically the accounts my father's set up for me and my siblings. He was telling me that the accounts have made very little money, if any - majority have lost money. My father has various additional accounts that, he opened on his own that have all done well. He's a busy guy who still works well over 80 hours a week, and has little time to research. What he knows he's learned on his own, and its commendable, but it's frustrating to know that the individual he's hired isn't making my father happy. With seeing so many shady reports of advisors not making the ROI that their clients expect while taking money off the top makes us leery.

Another victim tells his story -

I have had a financial advisor for almost 2 years. He charges me $750/yr to actively manage some stocks for me. In these 2 years, he has lost me $2k (out of $10k). Thats a total of $3.5k that I have lost since we started. I save around $6-7K a year.

These people have no recourse because brokerage house advisors are NOT fiduciary - they have no obligation to serve your best interests. If you want an advisor, get a fee-only FA. They are bound directly to you as a fiduciary duty. If they do not put your interests first (by you paying them a flat fee), then they are legally liable. Not so with a brokerage advisor. They are salespeople who have a responsibility to not give you bad advice while trying their best to make their brokerage money. They have split loyalties.

Skimming Your Savings

Remember, it's not 1% of profits; it's 1% of ASSETS. And on top of that, most brokers charge a load, which is basically taking a percentage of your assets upon entry or exit of a fund just because you are doing it on their advice. So, 1% of assets annually plus an immediate loss of (usually) 5% upon subscription or redemption. Meanwhile, investors who enter/leave the fund without the advice of a broker pay little to nothing, and possibly far less in annual fees.

This fellow has a disturbing story involving a celebrity financial adviser:

Back in 2008 ... I was listening to David Ramsey back then and decided to get with one of his "Endorsed Local Providers". Nice guy, seemed very religious and always with a smile on his face. After looking over my finances he said the best bet would be to transfer both mine and my wife IRAs to a Franklin and Templeton Front loaded mutual funds (Front load was 5.5% but I got a 2% discount for investing over 100k, I am sure he got a nice little kick-back for that). He on the other hand would manage my taxed account for a 1% annual fee.

What did I get for that? A 30% loss in my investments when the market tanked later that year (in fairness everybody was down). Looking back, the part that really bothered me though was that I had an extra $500 a month to invest (in addition to roth IRAs and 401k/TSP) and he had me invest it with him in the taxable account (instead of upping my TSP contributions I believe he did that so he can make more money from his 1% fee. In addition, he was buying and selling mutual funds every quarter which cost me a bunch of transaction fees. After three years of this I got wise and found the Boglehead philosophy and left him and moved to vanguard and use index funds. The decision to talk to the FA ended costing me upwards of 10k in fees over a 3 year period.

In the investing industry, the line between what's best for the client and what's good for the adviser is easily blurred. Sure an advisor wants big money for their client - it makes them look good, but they need a paycheck, too. The possibility of big commissions is there. Most clients have no idea what they're forking over and less idea how those charges kill their returns. People assume their FA is required to act in their interests, but the oversight committees (some of them are private, for-profit) do not require that at all. Ontario demands FA's act 'fairly, honestly, and in good faith.' There's a big gap from there to 'client interests come before advisor interest.' That's a fiduciary standard and it applies to accountants, for example, as well as lawyers.

When the Ontario Securities Commission hired (1994) Glorianne Stromberg to make recommendations, she returned with a blunt statement. "It's a travesty." She wanted to do away with the title 'investment advisor' and replace it with 'salesperson.' The provinces are trying to get the framework changed - Canada is quite bad about protecting people's interest against this industry. But the bank lobbies are very determined to hang onto this revenue stream - and they're one of the most powerful lobbies around.

The Grid is your Enemy

The 'grid' is the dark underbelly of the industry. Advisors get a percentage of their commission revenues and this percentage increases as their commission revenues increase. An advisor bringing in $500k will get about 35% of that, taking home $175,000. Over a million and the advisor takes home 50% or more - $500,000. Failing to meet the minimum will get the advisor pounding the pavement. The pressures are intense, as you can imagine. Sales must be made to keep the coffers filled. The client loses.

It's the way the industry is constructed and many advisors are not dishonest. They are just doing what they were trained to do - make money whether the client loses money or not. It's why I decided not to become an FA - although several large companies issued offers. I chose instead to simply offer straight investment advice privately.

Most clients actually trust their brokers (even if they're not totally loyal, they don't distrust them). However, they are not happy with their returns. They doubt their own skills at investing and analyzing and feel confused about recommended instruments. The clients cannot gage the value of the guidance. Many people actually believe their advisor works for free!

Most investors are rubes, it seems and have little to no idea that brokerage houses, even the big banks houses, charge substantial fees and get mutual fund kickbacks. Fair enough not knowing the details, but anyone who thinks a financial services company is giving them advice for free ought to check into the basic tenet of Adam Smith about lunches.

Often advisors get pushed to drop a well-performing fund and replace it solely to keep moving up the 'grid.' The fund sector is happy to comply, loading on closed-end funds for advisors to churn fees through and get an immediate kickback. The average Joe has no idea how they're being milked. One former investment exec noted a shocking reality - clients must make at least 5% and up to 8% just to break even with the fees. And that doesn't even factor in inflation.

And there are two types of fees just with mutual funds - the broker makes a cut when the trade is made. The company also gets to pocket some of the 1% AUM fee the mutual fund charges. And managers admit - off the record - these 'trailer fees' exist only to encourage brokers to sell them.

Often brokers are not even allowed to sell non-fee structured funds, even if they perform better. Any product without trailer fees will never find its way into a house's catalog.

Another scam is pushing new equity offerings. If a corporation wants financing from an investment bank, the execs will push down the equity by offering half the commission on the sale. It's usually around 4%, so if a deep pocket gets 'advice' to invest in a 'great new venture' by XYZ, he might shell out $500,000. Boom, financial advisor makes $10,000 for a few hours work finding the right sucker-client.

The problem is steadily worsening - the major banks have wealth management as a primary profit center. Scotia has moved from 3% to 20% of revenue from this center. Similar with other banks (at least in Canada). Changes will not come easily. There's just too much money at stake.

HOW YOUR FINANCIAL ADVISER GETS PAID

The grid: Many advisers are paid according to what's known as the grid, typically a one-page table that spells out how gross fees are shared between the adviser and their brokerage firm. The more fees the adviser brings in, the more of that cash they keep. An adviser generating fee and commission revenue of $200,000 a year might get to keep, say, 25 per cent. One earning $400,000 would get 35 per cent. Some brokers impose a minimum amount the adviser is expected to generate.

Fees: Some brokers charge an all-inclusive flat fee, typically in the range of 1 to 1.5 per cent, based on the size of your portfolio. A broker may also operate on a fee-for-service basis, either by the hour or based on the specific services they provide. Many other advisers offer what appears to "free" service, when in fact they are compensated via a vast array of fees on the investment products they put in your account. Many of these fees are not readily apparent to the investor.

Front-end sales or load commissions: You buy $10,000 of a mutual fund, and your adviser gets 2 per cent or $200. So your net purchase is actually $9,800.

Back-end or deferred fees: You buy a $10,000 mutual fund, $10,000 goes into your account and the adviser gets a commission. But sell that investment before a set period and you will be charged a fee.

Redemption fees: Paid by the investor to the fund when you sell units in a mutual fund.

Switch fees: Fee charged to investors when they switch funds within a family of funds.

Trailer fees: Annual fee the mutual fund pays your adviser and his or her firm to keep you in a particular fund. Rates are typically in the range of 0.25 per cent to 1 per cent a year.

Management Expense Ratios: This is the percentage of a mutual fund's assets that are deducted annually to cover operating costs, trailer fees, marketing, and fund manager salaries. MERs range from less than 1 per cent to 3 per cent or more. This comes right out of your return. So if a fund's investments generate a 5-per-cent return and the MER is 3 per cent, your return is about 2 per cent. Published returns are after fees are deducted.

Mr. Ross, a former mutual fund wholesaler, said brokers sometimes face pressure to dump the perfectly good funds already in a client's account in order to buy new ones, simply to generate fees needed to make their pay "grid." He said the mutual fund industry helps feed this thirst for income with a steady stream of new closed-end funds, which pay the broker up-front fees and may be sold at an initial discount to their book value to drive sales.

The public has no idea what's happening. The investor needs around 7% (or more) return just to break even!

Lies You will Hear

When the stakes are high, studies show that people are far more likely to deceive. Often this is in the form of cover-up or omission. One study showed that 100% of negotiators had omitted information because they were not asked directly about it. No financial advisor will tell you of their conflict of interest. If you knew, you would walk out the door immediately. It's virtually certain that you will not be told all you need to know in any negotiation.

You have almost definitely been deceived in negotiations in the past - problems with a new house, a job, or a business arrangement. You may have even 'fudged the data' yourself to gain a favorable outcome. Most people do. Several situations suggest a high likelihood of deceit - lots of money on the table; high potential losses; and an opposite negotiator with a poor reputation or poor negotiating skills. This can be countered with a firm and clear statement that all information will be fact-checked thoroughly.

If you want to know how your financial advisor is getting paid search the firm he or she works for. Next click "investment adviser firm" then the "SEC" link (in the US). This will pull up what's called a form ADV. On the left side it has the entire form organized in different parts. Click "Part 2 Brochures" under the Part 2 heading. This next page will give you links to PDF documents that explain the firms fee structures based on what kind of account you have open. It's buried pretty deep, and it's a mind-number, but it's there. Though a useful document, the best option would be to just call your advisor. Legally, he or she has to disclose all fees.

There are other, quite serious conflicts - not all of them built in to the pay structure conflict. For example, most of a financial advisor's time is spent trolling for new clients. That's how they pay the bills - by catching new fish. Goldman Sachs clients were infamously called 'muppets,' and while most houses are probably not that Machiavellian, it does show an extreme example of a general trend. Your well-being is not their top priority. Using your money to make money for them is the priority. It's really that simple. Your money is the leverage for their profits. How else could it be?

Restrictions

They also have bizarre regulatory restrictions that will put your portfolio in jeopardy. Woody O'Brien quit being a federally regulated broker. He was pressured by regulators, who said a regulated broker could not give advice about buying physical gold and silver. Why not, he wondered, if it meets their financial needs? He hung up the certificate and gave his advice - buy physical gold and silver.

A broker makes little to no money on your transaction if you purchase PM's. And he receives no ongoing fees for you owning it. So a broker may well be serving their own self-interest by advising you away from it, or advising limited purchases (10% of portfolio is occasionally recommended). He may advise you to invest in exchange traded metals funds to 'get exposure' to the metals' price. This is not ownership of PM's. It is ownership of an unallocated fund which does not specify title to any clear gold. Settlement can be in cash and getting the actual metals out will not be possible for the normal investor. Seasoned analysts have expressed many concerns about ETF's. Your broker may also steer you toward mining companies. These have the serious problem of share dilution (lowering value) and ease of manipulation, but your broker may get a nice fee for your purchase of them. So any broker who does advise you to go buy some coins at your local shop is probably considering your best interest - he gains nothing by it. In fact, he loses the cream from the money you take out of his control.

Even if they have some autonomy, money managers look for flash and ignore statistical performance. They see a company that has performed really well in the past year - and jump on the bandwagon. Sure, sometimes it pays off. But usually, it loses. Why? Because the company just went up on a statistical fluke. It wasn't a real boost. It was good marketing with no substance, or a viral hit that sent it soaring. After, they invest you, and ... the bird falls to earth with your money. It's a completely common scenario.

Peddling Insurance

All financial advisors must get their 'life insurance agent's license.' Their job is to sell you insurance - you could talk to a hundred commission based financial planners and every one will try to put you in several insurance products. They are not financial advisors - they are insurance salesmen. Many of them make their livelihood primarily from insurance. They receive residual income for each policy sold as long as the policy is in effect. Do you really need the line of insurance? They don't care. Will you buy insurance you don't need? - this is their question.

Insurance, for the most part, is a racket. Stories of non-payout on things people thought they were insured for are legion. Of course, they will pay on many claims, but the game is to pay off the small claims, then delay payment on big ones and lower the amounts or contest the claim altogether. Most people would be okay without the small claims anyway - the money they saved on insurance would more than cover these. And certainly many people are happy when they have a major claim and it is covered, but many more are not. After paying insurance for many years, they are left bereft with a denied claim.

After the advisor get the insurance license, it's a mutual fund license. Then they are licensed as financial advisors. If you want the worst performing investment in the market - the mutual fund - they can help. If you want carefully selected stocks - they can't.

No Legal Recourse for You

If you feel your FA has robbed you, you're probably right. But try and take them to court. You'll find out, in the fine print, that you can't. You've almost certainly agreed to arbitration, rather than court. This agreement forces you into a binding agreement based on an arbitrator's judgment. And guess who the arbitrator works for? Wall Street. Almost all the arbitrators have industry ties. They probably don't have a particular tie to your company, but they may. It may even be indirect.

They tend to have a policy of taking care of their own. After all, it might be the sued FA who sits on the arbitration board next go-round. Each financial firm wants to get the soft treatment, so they give it to the others. With nearly 5000 cases filed each year, the industry organization Finra and other industry trade groups insist the arbitration is to keep fees low and make disputes available to smaller investors. If so, why don't most agreements allow a dissatisfied client to take it to court? It protects the firm, that's why. The industry is arbitrating itself and experts say it's to the customers detriment. The process is tilted to the houses and it is non-transparent. There are many problems.

One study revealed that arbitrators rewards - when clients won - were significantly less than disputes handled by a disinterested regulator with no industry ties. If you find yourself in such an unfortunate situation - bring a lawyer. They usually get a better settlement. It could be good idea (consult a lawyer) to lay the evidence presented here to the arbitration board. They will issue a settlement with a non-disclosure agreement. Use this as leverage to increase the settlement. Otherwise, you can walk away and tell the papers - or write a book, blog, etc.

Arbitration is rigged. The attorney general of Minnesota brought suit against NAF - the privately owned, for-profit National Arbitration Forum. She demonstrated that the NAF was complicit with credit card companies and had strong financial ties to them while adjudicating the cases brought against those same companies - JP Morgan, Citigroup, Bank of America and the rest of the major banks. Lori Swanson - the AG - laid charges of defrauding the public. The credit card companies owned the NAF outright through a shell company. The NAF, posing as an independent arbitrator, was used as an arm of the debt collection agency. The clauses in the card agreements precluded any right to trial by jury - the arbitration was binding. It clearly violated consumer rights and the 7th amendment. Arbitrators were given instructions on how to rule by the companies. If they ruled against the defendant, they would lose their position on the arbitration board.

The primary tactic is simply to use a pocketed arbitrator. In one network, a paltry 28 arbitrators handled 90% of the caseload - 19,500+ cases total. These arbitrators found for the corporate party 95% of the time, with the highest case numbers going to the arbitrator finding for the company the highest percent. It's called the 'repeat player' problem in arbitration.

The Public Investors Arbitration Bar Association found that the National Association of Securities Dealers had rigged the computer selection system, favoring arbitrators who ... well, you know. The firm first robs people of the retirement savings, then cheats them in a forced arbitration panel by stacking the 'neutral' panel against them.

Arbitrators are not bound to follow legal code. Any ruling is in fact, legal. It may not be binding if you can manage to get it in court, but that is difficult with the legal clauses put in place by the financial and securities dealers.

One analyst threw it at the Supreme Court - arbitration cases were awarded in favor of the banks 99.6% of the time. Another problem - arbitration fees could be thousands of dollars upfront, precluding almost all smaller cases. And you still lose. The Supreme Court didn't care about the evidence. They ruled in favor of arbitration, ignoring the majority of evidence. If your financial advisor screws you, you will have no legal recourse.

How is your FA getting paid? Commissions, other fees, etc.

The majority of FA's use the broker-dealer pattern - consulting with you and getting paid through various charges overlaid on your account. A huge number of conflicts of interest result from this arrangement - costing you $1000's (note the plural) of dollars each year. One problem - most FA's are trained to pile up assets, not to professionally manage your funds. More and bigger piles of assets equals greater fees for them - from you. More and more transactions generated, more revenue for them - from you. Even a child could see the conflict - but most middle net worth investors are blind.

It's a broad-ranging systemic reality. It exists only because the earliest companies did it the same way - a century and half ago! Have things changed? Sure - a lot. Markets are a lot less opaque, a lot more liquid, and individuals have easy access to trading platforms, especially in the last 7 or 8 years. The most ethical, well-meaning FA's must use this system -which works against you - to make more money. Contrariwise, they can take on more clients, but then they can't give you as much attention.

With a commission and fee-based structure, FA's have a big incentive to sell you things you probably don't need. And since the commission is only a fraction of the cost of the product, you have to invest a lot to float them. That money is market exposure - which can be good, but is often a very bad approach to the market. The most profitable traders with lowest risk have the most minimal market exposure - many of them close every trade by the end of every day.

But the cream of the cream of advisors are NOT those who do best for clients - it is those who do best for themselves and their company. No award and no recognition are given for 'excellent client service' or even 'top returns to clients.'

It gets worse. Many companies peg you for AUM - the assets under their management. It's a screw job for most investors. If you have an average net worth ($50k to $2 million), you should be awfully concerned about this model. The fees for AUM vary from half a percent to 2.5% - with the lower end (below $1 million) paying the highest.

If you have $1 million, you're getting tagged for almost $12.5grand - plus other charges. This is a huge fee considering most people are not satisfied with their FA. Less than 15% of the wealthy are loyal even though most FA's believe their clients are loyal.

If your FA does not disclose in total transparency how he gets paid, whether by AUM or commissions or both - you are doing business with the wrong person.

When all is added up, fees are usually about 2% of managed assets. Posit $10k base investment for 50 years. If the market gives 7% average return, that adds up to $295k (give or take). If you dish out 2% per year to your manager, you'll get back 5%. That same $10k yields only $115k - or a jaw-dropping 70% less. The managers are causing you to LOSE lots of money.

Pile on top the fact that the funds underperform the indexes and you're losing even more.

Why is your FA recommending what he does?

The FA typically covers a range of issues and news with clients - politics, various sectors and the overall economy. This is the source of most advisements, but these lead to numerous trades from which the adviser collects fees.

Your losses exceed 35% just from fees every year. That's if you have an average risk tolerance. If your portfolio is half equities and half bonds, then you probably get about 5% per year return (unless you take a loss from a major drawdown like 2008). Most funds charge around 1% and the AUM fees are up to 1.5% - 2.5% total. Factor that into the return and you're left with a scant 50% roughly.

Are your FA's suggestions up to the minute, well-explained, and comprehensible? Do you feel good about them considering the associated fees?

Should your FA have group pow-wows including all clients to honestly discuss the pros and cons of the decisions? Can you conceive of such a thing and how it might truly benefit clients?

How do you know you're getting placed in instruments that benefit you the most?

Advisors have a big motive (money) to put your money into specific funds - namely the ones that generate the highest fees for them. Many of these funds are front-load fees - they charge you money to get into the fund, on top of the management fees. Your broker gets some of this money and there's no extras you get. The funds are not better for you.

All commission houses have a book of favored partners operating funds. The broker has a profit sharing deal going on with the fund. Your broker could pocket a couple of grand each year just for keeping you in a favored fund. Do you think he wants you in a cheap fund that doesn't fill his wallet? Probably not, even though it would be in your interest.

The venerable firm Edward Jones (my mother's firm, btw) was tagged in 2011 for a $75 million fine for just such a scheme and noted on record that it was a conflict of interest. But they kept right on, collecting over $150 million the following year from revenue sharing.

They even hide the information (in plain 'site' naturally.) It's buried in a sunken web-layer inside a mountain of other tedious and sleepy data. The fact that you're paying substantial fees without express knowledge is not interesting enough to disclose in a clear, straightforward manner. This practice is ubiquitous in the FA sector. It's just how business is done.

Does your FA push you to 'get' the approach he's laying out for my savings?

What is your time horizon? When do you begin drawing down money, how much will be paid in, etc.

What is your risk tolerance? If you lose a lot of value suddenly, will you freak out?

What is your present allocation of assets? It's critical to analyze the various factors in your immediate allocation in order to proceed with a plan.

He should also discuss other issues - especially inflation and the ongoing currency and economic problems and trade wars plaguing the various economies.

Consider the following in light inflation, for example.

Currently inflation is relatively low - 2% CPI and 9% by better measures (more on that in the inflation section. But with the Federal Reserve's activity lately, inflation is 'baked in the cake.' Potentially extremely high inflation and an eventual devaluation of the dollar. How will this affect your portfolio? Has your advisor warned you of the probability of another serious crisis?

When inflation is running hot, it is extremely difficult to maintain a positive real return - inflation adjusted, that is. In other words, you may be making some money nominally, but you are losing purchasing power. Considering that the Fed doctors the inflation rate to keep it low - for several reasons - you are almost definitely losing real value.

Even worse - quite a few advisors do not care about your tax burden - they may not even understand it. They don't put your eggs in the lower cost brackets and large return stocks can cost you the normative tax rate. Now some people swear by IRA's and 401(k)'s, but I don't think these are all they're cracked up to be long-term. There is a certain risk of government 'confiscation.'

Not that Uncle S. will take them outright - they will simply be forced into debt instruments. You'll become the proud holder of a fistful of US Treasuries at the worst interest rates in history. And looking down the barrel of a sinking dollar.

Does your firm have a developed, knowledgeable team that will see your portfolio through the challenges?

Few people, even the wealthy (but not uber-wealthy - above $10 million) feel they receive enough input and advice on meeting their financial goals. Most FA's contact clients when they want to sell them something (for commission). It could be insurance, stocks, mutual funds, etc. They also pick up the horn when the market rolls over and you take a loss. They're worried about you taking your business to somebody that can better protect your ass(ets!) And they should be, because you should probably leave most FA's.

Is your FA a fiduciary?

A fiduciary is legally obligated to place your interests ahead of their own. If they fail in this responsibility - by churning your portfolio and collecting profits to your detriment - they can be held accountable. Churning is a common tactic, whereby FA's simply by and sell lots of fund shares to collect commissions - and you pay the commission each trade.

Is your FA an insurance Pusher?

I know of many advisors who simply sell lines of insurance. These are billed to clients as necessities for financial protection - home insurance, life insurance, catastrophic illness, etc. Now, there's nothing inherently wrong with insurance. Trouble is, you're probably not in very good product lines. If a seriously high claim is filed, you may very well find yourself unpaid or fighting it in court, or worse, in arbitration rigged against you. Also, the advisor gets paid a percentage of your insurance premium, month after month, as long as you have the policy. Many advisors push high-commission lines with scare tactics and load their clients up with excessive numbers of policies that are totally unnecessary, just to get the commission.

It's part of the rig - FA's typically have to get their insurance license first, then their mutual fund license. That's not because you're best served by buying lines of insurance and mutual fund shares - it's because the company gets money from you doing this. Oftentimes, they are the insurer, so of course they want to sell policies. But they disguise it as financial protection. It's not really, or only minimally. It's a largely unnecessary product they scare you into buying.

What are your FA's product fees?

Some FA's will tell you their products have no fees. This is a lie, but they will phrase it as a not-lie, or an omission. In other words, if you get 'guaranteed 2.5%' rate, they will say there are no fees lowering that 2.5% - you get the full amount. The omission is that the fees are already calculated and the annuity pays 4% - and 1.5% goes to your FA and his company.

Warning! Alert! The Rigging of the Market

This market intervention and manipulation has fostered the greatest-ever speculation in global securities markets, which has motivated only greater central control . . . central bankers believe that they have no choice but to dominate markets—to dominate seemingly everything ~Doug Noland, Federated Investors

There is a very serious issue with your investments that your FA will never, ever mention. He will deny it scornfully if you ask. He probably does not believe it himself and thinks the idea is a 'conspiracy.' The markets are heavily manipulated. If a well-funded group can move a market for profits - do you think it will? Certainly some will, especially if they are safe from prosecution. As we will see, they are. The US Department of Justice (and equivalent bodies in other countries) have written official policy that very large financial institutions will not be prosecuted. They've even been caught in multiple arenas (LIBOR, gold, derivatives) - yet ask your FA about market manipulation by the major commercial investment banks and he will likely scoff.

When something as critical to your portfolio as market manipulation is shown on the front page of every major newspaper in the world, and most advisors deny it - something is wrong. You are in serious danger. You absolutely cannot invest in manipulated markets safely. And if you don't know about the manipulation - you will lose money. Of course, the current reason for manipulation is to make everyone think they markets are fine. They're

40

goosed by the Fed to placate the public. And everyone makes money - until they don't. Until the bottom drops out and they lose big.

Equities and the bull market beliefs are separating from the very serious risks of capital markets - currency crises, liquidity, destructive printing, trade wars, real wars, massive indebtedness, and so forth). The true economy is stumbling yet stocks are rising. It's a recipe for a disaster, but the Plunge Protection Team keeps pushing the markets higher. They mostly seem to do it by buying S&P futures - a topic beyond this book, but quite interesting in its own right.

This manipulated separation is nowhere more clear than in Blackrock's 2015 Investment Outlook:

Corporate earnings are a key risk. Analysts predict double-digit growth in 2015, yet such high expectations will be tough to meet. Companies have picked the low-hanging fruit by slashing costs since the financial crisis. How do you generate 10% earnings-per-share growth when nominal GDP growth is just 4%?

It becomes tempting to take on too much leverage, use financial wizardry to reward shareholders or even stretch accounting principles. S&P 500 profits are 86% higher than they would be if accounting standards of the national accounts were used, Pelham Smithers Associates notes. And the gap between the two measures is widening, the research firm finds.

Analysts are more than happy to use the non-GAAP estimates for earnings - it lets them predict a bull market which the Fed has managed to maintain. GAAP means Generally Accepted Accounting Principles, but they're just so... pre-crisis. Companies don't really use them anymore for public relations and market news, especially since an Executive Order from the oval office made it legal to ignore correct accounting. Now FAAP - Fudged Awful Accounting Principles are the 'new normal.' Everybody's doing it.

The consensus estimate for EPS (earning per share) is 126. If we use Black Rock's revisions (and Black Rock is probably the best investment company in the world by actual performance metrics), the EPS is below 70. And that means that next year's Price/Earnings (the widest used measure of corporate value) is actually 30. 15 is the accepted ratio of good value for an established company. The biggest companies in the world, so-called blue chips, are overvalued by 100%! But that's the perpetual market lie to keep you in the game. Ask you FA if he's aware of this very unsettling con game in the markets. Odds are he hasn't a clue. And if he does, why is he still recommending those same companies and calling it 'value investing?'

Fact is, central banks cannot close the distance between the bull frenzy bubbles in the equities markets and the steady decline of the consumer economies. Yet they are connected. These companies rely on the consumer for actual income, so P/E (stock price to earnings) ratios are becoming increasingly strained, and often manipulated. Increased printing and goosing of markets only worsens the divide, leading to a greater 'systemic risk.' The attempt to reflate the system cannot work in the long run - it is not getting money into Main Street pockets, only onto bank balance sheets. Central Banks are actually selling/printing systemic risk. At some point the gap will close suddenly and painfully in an unpredictable manner. There may be a stock market mother of all crashes. Or there may be a repudiation of the Reserve currencies - US Dollar, British Pound, and Euro - that will lead to massively inflationary, possibly hyperinflationary outcome.

The 'new normal' is characterized by a mega-bubble, rather than a sector bubble. Whereas before, bubbles were in dotcom or mortgage securities, now the majority of the financial arena is in a bubble - almost all asset sectors are at unrealistic valuations. Previous bubbles were measured in the hundreds of billions to a few trillion. Now we are looking at a multi-hundred trillion dollar asset bubble ranging across all assets. Junk bonds, Interest Rate Swaps, stocks, Treasuries, even currencies - all are in a bubble. When the whirling dervish of instruments spins itself into pieces, we will experience a result no one ever has and no one can anticipate. The world will be different.

From 2000-13 on an inflation adjusted basis, the stock market was flat. (It's now emerged past that, due to upward manipulation). And that's with the government inflation numbers, which are manipulated to make the government look good (or less bad.) Even the idea that the Dow Jones is at the same level (or higher) than it was years ago is a bit flawed for several reasons. First, the survivor bias is critical. Any stock below a specific share price is replaced in the index! Comparing the Dow today to the Dow ten years ago is apples to oranges. It means that some of the companies got so weak, they were cut. The Dow would be several hundred points lower if it were the same today as in 2001. Since it's used as a proxy for the health of the entire market, it's an important problem.

It fails to account for the growth, death and capital base of corporations. The number of public companies declined by 50% between 1997 and 2010. The stock market is actually a slaughterhouse. In many cases, the capital flowed into larger companies, but mostly, the money was simply lost to investors as companies went belly-up. The abuses of HF Traders has diminished desirability in the stock market. Most slow money investors don't want to be there - they don't want to be prey. The big money, the smart money - has left. Only institutional money remains, invested in HFT. But they close out ALL positions every day, so they aren't really invested in the market per se. They're more like an exploding batch of leeches on the market, sucking the blood out of it - and most middle class portfolios. They are invested in very sophisticated market derivatives, and you don't access to those.

The stock market is held up by the President's Working Group on Financial Markets - the so-called Plunge Protection Team. They buoy the markets artificially. They use tricky methods like layering - stacking up orders - spoofing - dropping a monster order, then retracting it - and quote stuffing - a method to create phantom orders. This created a false market depth so that very elite HFT firms could attack each other.

Some very well-informed designers, the so-called plumbers who built the systems, in the HFT field have warned of a possible market attack by China or other enemy governments in the trade wars. This would create a massive crisis and possibly a system collapse. Velocity, cleverness, innovation, manipulation, hiddenness are the keys to today's stock market. Value investing is dead.

In fact, at this writing, the world's wealthiest investors and executive insiders are shoveling off their shares at an unprecedented pace. Soros has cut loose more than one million shares of the mega-banks. Buffet has jettisoned even J&J and Kraft. The % allocated to consumer goods is below 23% - a new low dip. Paulson, who won big predicting the 2007-8 subprime fiasco, is dropping even Family Dollar - typically considered a recession proof stock.

The markets have devolved from any semblance of value investing - searching for underpriced stocks with good earnings and low share price - to a game of frontrunning the surges of Fed liquidity and secret buying binges. This is a dangerous game and it cannot go on forever. The imbalances become too great, the heroin need from capital markets starts to poison the capital market corpus. Each fresh infusion will be bigger and badder than the previous, but each time it will have less effect. The law of diminishing returns will take hold.

It will not be completely obvious, perhaps. It may come in the form of a massive crash, but the Fed can stop that, or reverse it in a day or so. They have and will do so again. (I suggest buying long Out of the Money, near term call spreads for cheap right after a serious crash. The Fed WILL goose the markets right back to where they were.) The damage will be to the dollar itself. The market will not really crash, but the real value of the market will be a LOT less due to massive dollar depreciation.

There are ways to make money off this sudden event (or gradual), but you must be nimble and VERY skilled. Most ordinary investors will lack the market understanding to trade options on this situation for profit - and that's the real way to make good money. It's also a real way to LOSE good money. But the opportunities will be there.

At any rate - the market is grievously overvalued at present. The Fed is backstopping it and the investment community is solely relying on infusions of liquidity to keep the market 'toppy' in perpetuity.

Transfers from Main St to Wall St

On almost any metric the US equity market is historically quite expensive. . . . Can we say when it will end? No. Can we say that it will end? Yes. And when it ends and the trend reverses, here is what we can say for sure. Few will be ready. Few will be prepared ~ Seth Klarman, Baupost Group

In a secret meeting, Ben Bernanke told a group of bankers that the Fed would support a troubled sector of the market. Those execs made bets accordingly and won a ton of money. How can you compete against such favored information. And if you think this was a one-time occurrence, it is not. This is the norm.

There is an adage - the stock market exists to transfer money from Main Street to Wall Street. The story of Priceline stock illustrates this nicely. The former CEO of Priceline received options for the stock of several hundred thousand shares as part of his compensation. He exercised these options at $20 to $30 per share. Options, of course, are not exercised at market prices, but at pre-agreed prices. These insider shares are created when the options are exercised, as if they were new shares. When options are exercised, the buyer gets the shares at the option price, not the market price. He can then sell them at the market price. When Boyd exercised the options, he was able to sell the new shares into the market at more than $550/share. This 2000% windfall put $120 million in his pocket. The Priceline stock began tanking soon afterwards. It was the second time this had happened. Priceline went to a high of $960/share in the early 2000s. Then, after some option exercises, it fell to $6. About 20% of the ownership is from Vanguard, Fidelity and other 401(k) funds. Financial advisory companies used retirement monies to unload insider stocks - up to a billion - on Priceline. The funds inflated the value of the stock from $300 million to $30 billion, by encouraging the public to invest in this company. In other words, After inflating the value of Priceline stock, they then sold off private stock options at that price, draining off the public investment. As the saying goes, the stock market transfers money from Main Street to Wall Street.

Goldman Sach, for example, rode both sides of the merger when the electronic trading network Archipelago merged with the New York Stock Exchange. G-Sax had seats on both parties worth millions, then tens of millions afterward. They negotiated the deal - a massive conflict of interest ignored by regulators. Indeed, conflicts of interest have become SOP - standard operating procedure. Nobody cares because of a little problem called regulatory capture - where the companies get their people in the 'watchdog' organization. It's also called self-regulating industries. Well, it should work out best for everybody, right? Or...not.

Along a different line, one financial advisor mistake is nearly ubiquitous - investing in the well-known CEO's companies. FA's love to do this, because they must be famous for a reason - like they're really good at what they do. But it just ain't so. Most famous CEO's are just good at getting media attention. Overconfident CEO's and celebrity CEO's do very poorly in research. They often make catastrophically risky gambles which lose lots of money. They are locked into a need to appear to know everything or being replaced. They must make bad bets on limited knowledge in the interests of job security. Thus their interests are in direct conflict with other stakeholders.

VXX is the poster child of Wall Street selling nothing for something. This scam is a bet on volatility and tracks - sort of - the VIX. The VIX is a measure of volatility based on the options of the S&P 500. As they get more expensive, the market is getting nervous and charging more for them. But you can only trade VIX options and futures - not the VIX directly. So the VXX was created to track the VIX and invest directly. It was issued by Barclay's and has lost 99% since then. If the instrument is reverse split adjusted back to its inception date, it began at $7000 and is now at $30. Barclay's issued a lot more shares of VXX when it rolled it out - now there are 43 million. As the original price dropped, the shares were 'reverse split' or combined to bring the value of a single share back up to $100. At any rate, the original issue was worth around $300 billion - all going to Barclay's and taken out of the market, btw.

Barclay's will redeem those shares when it closes the fund - around 2018. By current price, the market cap (shares times price) is worth about $1.3 billion. Barclays has realized a monstrous profit on this instrument - which carries nothing of value and nothing productive. It is merely a poor means of tracking market volatility with a pricing mechanism causing a steady decline. There are about 30 of these funds just tracking volatility. Not to mention numerous other such paper ETF's that simply track the price of a commodity or basket of stocks (like the SPY which tracks the S&P). Add these up and the banks are simply draining the markets of otherwise productive capital. They are also taking your investment money in a steady drain. Not to mention, the banks get the money upfront and pay a tiny share of it back in 15 years. Or never if the fund is not going to be redeemed.

These are some of the many scams perpetrated on the middle class by the finance class. But these are just sneaky ways of vacuuming the money in a steady stream. There is a much worse, and completely legal, way that The Street already uses your own assets against you. They will sell your assets that are under their care.

Stock Buybacks

One of the great, unspoken schemes going on in 2014 to 2015 is stock buybacks - when a company buys its stock on the open market. Now, there's nothing inherently wrong with stock buybacks. In fact, it can be a sign of financial strength. If a company is doing well enough to buy massive shares of its own stock, it must be flush with capital. Hold on - that may not be the case at all.

Stock buybacks have become a means of robbing Peter to pay Paul - in multiple ways. First, the connected insiders are dumping personal shares at an unheard of rate. That means they distrust the long-term strength of the company. They know share prices should be lower - no matter what P/E ratios say. P/E is price to earnings, or share price X shares outstanding divided by annual money the company earns. Usually a P/E of 15 is decent and lower is better (unless it goes negative which means that earnings are negative because share price cannot be.) What's the take-away? Insiders are using company funds to bolster the price so they can sell off their shares at max profit. Later, when they're done, the stock will inevitably drop, often quite fast. It may come with a general market downturn, but it will come. They are kicking investors to the curb. It's actually a criminal offense on multiple counts, but it's so hard to make that stick it will never see an investigation.

That's not all. Some companies are actually floating out bond debt to do buybacks. This looks great in the market - which is all most people can see. It gives a huge favor to short-term investors and traders. But it decays the balance sheet. Corporate financials go downhill even as the stock price rises. It's a basic manipulation and guess who loses? YOU. Ask your FA if he knows anything about these schemes.

Rehypothecation - How they legally own everything you think you own

Get out now! ~ Ann Barnhardt, Barnhardt Capital Management

You don't own your stock certificates. The DTCC actually owns your stock certificates. Depositary Trust and Clearing Corporation is the largest company you've never heard of. Virtually all stock transfers and sales pass through this company. It handles trillions of dollars on a daily basis. And - it owns your stocks. You technically have an IOU saying that they will give you your stock upon request. They're holding it for you.

Urban lingo has the phrase OPM - other people's money. Banks have developed the art of OPM to the utmost degree. It should really be called other people's assets because they would hardly stop at mere money. The technique is called rehypothecation. Rehypothecation (and it's out of control younger sibling 'hyper-hypothecation') tells all about the moral direction and free reign of bankers. It's also the slow strangulation of the middle class.

Hypothecation is simply the use of an asset as collateral. Rehypothecation is the use of client assets by a brokerage or financial firm as collateral for the firm's purposes. The client takes the risk and the firm gets the reward. The asset is still owned by the original party, but it is 'hypothetically' controlled by the lender. While it can be compensated, most clients are unaware of the procedure and their assets are used without their knowledge. Of course, it's in the fine print, but it's seldom clear. Usually, it's used against the client - equities are borrowed for short sales against the securities, driving the price down. It begs the question - who owns the assets in a default scenario, the client or the entity with collateral pledged to it? Collateral has no meaning except to secure a loan in the case of default. If your stock is collateralized for MS to borrow money from JPM, then you can actually lose your assets when MS hits the skids and 'The Morgue' collects its collateral. This happened with MF Global and PFG Best. Numerous investors got skinned.

Rehypothecation has different limits in different places. In the US, 140% of the value can be loaned against. In the UK, there is no limit. Client collateral can be used again and again to finance more speculation. London is the banker's paradise for a very clear reason. Rehypothecation is very profitable, so all the big houses set up a London office to milk the cow as hard as possible - relocating client assets without their knowledge to the UK. Half the shadow system was based on rehypothecation by 2007. It was not on balance sheets for several reasons. Not being cash, it didn't have to be there. But it was a good cash substitute and a great way to make money. This surged up capital to earnings ratios - a hidden way of looking stronger. It looked as if companies made very high returns for capital, but it hid the massive leverage being used. It's not pretty either. Up to four times leverage is based on awful collateral. Even Reuters printed, "Considering that re-hypothecation may have increased the financial footprint of Eurozone bonds by at least four fold then a Eurozone sovereign default could be apocalyptic."

Before Lehman collapsed, the collateral was about $1 trillion, while the rehypothecation was about $4 trillion. Afterwards, hedge funds balked at the risk and put clauses limiting or preventing the practice into place. Now only 'muppets' - average investors who don't know better - have their assets put on the block.

Singh and Aitken showed that rehypothecation played a central role in the 2008 crisis and subsequent deleveraging. This led to a drying of credit and disappearance of lending between banks and in the general economy. Markdowns on collateral - called 'margin spiral' - can rapidly get out of hand. Most of the asset backed mortgage instruments lost up to 90% of face value in months. The shadow banking system was much larger than previously understood - leading to a distorted, under-evaluation of systemic risk. Rehypothecation allows for pretty shady accounting. Multiple companies can list assets, unlike on-balance sheet assets. The differences in limits between the US and UK has also led to moving accounts to London primarily for the purpose of increasing hypothecation.

MF Global was a derivatives (options, futures, etc.) broker and a primary bond dealer for the US Treasury. This is an important point. Primary dealers are among the most scrutinized of financial companies. They are supposed to be very conservative in operation, extremely stable, and possess very high integrity - guaranteed by the regulatory authorities. This company was officially rated triple gold star, completely immune to any solvency and liquidity issues. The lesson is clear - the auditing system is broken. All parties failed in their duties - MF Global was highly leveraged, very risk-prone, and engaged in a number of unscrupulous practices. Clients, including subsidiary clients, lost billions.

Why the checks and balances system failed is less clear. It was either incompetence or willful deception. These are some of the highest paid accounting firms in the world. Either they got to their position through years and years of incompetence, it was a show of one-time incompetence, or they were deliberately and well-paid to do exactly what they did - cover up a financial black hole. How many more MF Globals are out there?

In 2008, the company got a $10 million fine for inappropriate trading activity, blaming it on a 'rogue trader,' a recurrent theme in the modern financial world. Liquidity concerns tanked the stock price, then it got another $10 million in fines for bad risk management. The company rehypothecated big-time, betting the farm on Greek debt. The debt was very high-yield. The firm took out credit default swaps on the bonds, probably hoping for a default with a subsequent massive payout by the swaps contracts. Timing was bad and the hyper-leverage dovetailed with market concerns - liquidity disappeared for MF Global. To maintain the appearance of solvency and liquidity, they dipped into the customer till. Segregated accounts are (were) considered sacrosanct. It was a line even the banks wouldn't cross. If they did, the system would have been exposed as hopelessly corrupt. Taking customer funds without asking is simply stealing, even if the intent is to return the funds. On October 31, 2011, the company admitted that $891 million in customer funds was transferred to cover huge losses, including an odd $175 million transfer directly to JP Morgan. The true amount is not well-disclosed, nor is the length of time the malpractice occurred. The amount was later adjusted to 'at least $1.6 billion.'

MF Global was using a complicated internal and external trade. Their London branch was doing a repo with the New York branch taking the other side - the reverse repo. A repo is a short-term sale with an agreement to buy back later. Repos are supposed to fund short-term liquidity needs, but they also allow for funny accounting games. The company used a fiction - an internal repo to maturity - to game the regulations. It was a simple one to spot, but the regulators ignored it. In this case, it was to provide a booked profit to make the business look more solvent. But the trade had a two-day shortfall in the window before maturity when the bonds were sold externally. This, combined with the default risk, put an unendurable liquidity crunch on the business. This became public knowledge, investors withdrew funds, lenders pulled back, and the death-spiral sank the ship, disappearing $1.6 billion, at last count, in client funds.

Analyst Chris Whalen calls it outright theft. Clients lost gold, bonds, currency and other assets. HSBC even filed suit against JP Morgan over $850,000 in gold held from MF Global. MF Global seems to have been pledging client gold - the ultimate backstop asset - against its creditors' claims. There would be no lawsuit between two such entities otherwise. This leads to a nasty potential revelation. If one is doing it, usually they all are. Again and again, this is proved - like in the LIBOR rigging. The question is whether and how much of the GLD and SLV exchange traded funds (HSBC is the custodian) are backed by physical gold. The metals can be rehypothecated to more than their market value. It may have multiple claims, and with the wording of the funds, the clients will be last in line. These funds are the biggest privately held stocks of silver and gold in the world.

Lehman and Bear Stearns were larger than the MF Global crisis. Customers were made whole in both cases before any other proceedings. This shows the extent of systemic strain at this point. Customer accounts are now needed to feed the beast. It exposes the problem in public view. Trust is beginning to fall off the cliff, which the mega-banks have wanted to avoid. They need to the money to stay where it is - on their ledgers - to keep leverage from upending their balance sheets. It's proof of desperation. And, in a footnote of corruption, the customers are being charged storage fees on their stolen metals - otherwise they forfeit any settlement claims on them in future. Meantime, the prices of the metal dropped precipitously, so the cash settlement was far less. And naturally, the assets were frozen, preventing the legitimate owners from selling them.

Commingling of funds is the ultimate crime in brokerage activities. No one was prosecuted. Ann Barnhardt closed down her financial firm based on the handling of MF Global, with the following letter, edited for brevity:

Barnhardt Capital Management has ceased operations... I could no longer tell my clients that their monies and positions were safe in the futures and options markets – because they are not. And this goes not just for my clients, but for every futures and options account in the United States. The entire system has been utterly destroyed by the MF Global collapse.

The futures markets are very highly-leveraged and thus require an exceptionally firm base upon which to function. That base was the sacrosanct segregation of customer funds from clearing firm capital, with additional emergency financial backing provided by the exchanges themselves. Up until a few weeks ago, that base existed, and had worked flawlessly.

Jon Corzine STOLE the customer cash at MF Global. ...[Regulators'] reaction has been to take a bad situation and make it orders of magnitude worse. Specifically, they froze customers out of their accounts WHILE THE MARKETS CONTINUED TO TRADE, refusing to even allow them to liquidate. ...The risk exposure precedent ... has destroyed the entire industry paradigm.

...MF Global is almost certainly the mere tip of the iceberg. The Chicago Mercantile Exchange did not immediately step in to backstop the MFG implosion because they knew and know that if they backstopped MFG, they would then be expected to backstop all of the other firms in the system when the failures began to cascade – and there simply isn't that much money in the entire system. In short, the problem is a SYSTEMIC problem, not merely isolated to one firm.

...The futures and options markets are no longer viable. ...The system is no longer functioning with integrity and is suicidally risk-laden. The rule of law is non-existent, instead replaced with godless, criminal political cronyism.

1.42 million ounces of silver went missing in the scandal - vaporized funds, the mainstream media called it. But it went somewhere, to someone. It was stolen. The bad bets, Jim Willie explained, put pressure on the Comex. People wanted delivery of their silver futures contracts. JP Morgan could not fulfill these contracts legally. "JPM increased the amount of silver in their registered vaults by precisely the amount that was supposed to be delivered...JPM effectively averted both a Comex default and a European Sovereign Debt implosion."

On Dec. 12, 2011, HSBC filed a lawsuit to prevent an MFGlobal client from taking delivery on physical gold and silver from the Comex. The metals were doubly owned, confirming the critics claims. It's difficult to sort out what really happened - probably by intent. MF Global lost precious metals it was supposed to deliver. JPMorgan apparently was being hammered by margin calls on a number of derivative bets getting out of hand. Their reserves were scraping bottom. The silver and gold futures calls for delivery had put the bank in a tight squeeze. They held onto the MFGlobal metals that were supposed to be sent, putting them into their own account.

JP Morgan is serving as trustee for the case in spite of their notable interest - they have liens on substantial assets. This conflict of interest is a spit in the eye of the clients. "Evidence mounts," Jim Willie explains, "that JPMorgan simply converted 614k ounces of MF Global client silver into JPM licensed vaults." Two definitions - eligible means that it meets quality standards for good delivery but is still owned by a private party. Registered means it is available for delivery to satisfy a futures contract. They moved 613,738 eligible ounces into their vaults on Nov. 18. After waiting a week, they changed it to registered. All the silver they held for others soon after the MF Global collapse was converted to JP Morgan ownership.

On Oct. 31st, MF Global publicly filed bankruptcy. The CME made a statement about 1.4 million ounces of silver vanished from the client holdings at MF Global. 627,182 was from banks outside the cartel. It was the first deposit in half a year of any quantity for JP Morgan into their silver vaults. The futures contracts (covered later), are many times the deliverable amount of silver available. The chart tells all you need to know - there is a massive decline in available silver for delivery. The Comex is approaching a default. They badly needed silver to meet futures deliveries, which are rising aggressively.

One trader, whose account was vaporized, said the freeze came because of stock positions with impossible counterparty risk. To save a few hundred accounts, the holdings of 35,000 commodities customers were stolen. Customer account receipts were immediately confiscated at the beginning of the investigation. This made it very difficult for them to prove their asset claims. The claim was that the money was missing and could not be found. US regulators accepted this even when it was shown to be a lie. Richard Heis, an administrator of MF Global's UK division, said, in the US the claim is "nobody knows where the money is. We know exactly where the money is." Some analysts claim the regulators are throwing up a dust cloud to protect the perpetrators, ticking the clock until the statute of limitations expires.

The 2005 bankruptcy reform act elevates derivatives above all other asset classes in a bankruptcy. This puts the banks (holders of 99% of all derivatives) above any other asset holder. In a rehypothecation scenario, the innocent public is pushed underwater and loses. Considering derivatives tower above all other assets by volume, the danger is extreme. In a true derivative havoc situation, no brokerage-held asset would appear to be safe - MF Global proves it. People would do well to examine the fine print in their pension and 401(k) contracts. If people have cash in an investment account at Morgan Stanley, for example, when the firm goes Lehman, that cash can be used legally to pay off MS's exploded derivatives. There is even a clawback provision. If the client removed the funds in the weeks beforehand, they can reverse the transfer.

When Bank of America took over Merrill Lynch, they bought a freakish $53 trillion in derivatives onto their balance sheet. By moving that and a pre-existing position ($77 trillion) from the investment to the commercial side, they put it on the FDIC's insurance list. According to the Market Ticker, it's an "armed financial nuclear device... daring anyone to tamper with it." All banks have the same type of massive systemic risk, deliberately booby-trapping their balance sheet. This is commingling on an extreme scale - the firewall between investments of a bank and client deposits is gone. The public is held hostage to the potential chaos. Bank CEO's, the Ticker claims, lie with impunity about the risks. The warning is very clear - "you could lose everything in your bank and investment accounts - every single dime."

The CME (Chicago Mercantile Exchange) is a non-governmental regulatory body in charge of overseeing MF Global and other such brokerages. Top management wrote a public letter in July, 2012. The group was "appalled by the recent misuse of segregated funds." In order to reinstate customer confidence, they proposed revised regulations, including unannounced audits of segregated funds, daily and bi-monthly reporting and electronic confirmations of segregated funds, and CEO guarantees of procedures. "CME Group is committed to making whatever changes are necessary to strengthen customer protections, restore confidence in the futures industry and ensure the effectiveness of these critical markets."

Unfortunately, the CME reneged on this mission even before the letter. They had an agreement to make investors whole as part of their mandate, but refused to do so. They probably had the money, but according to the organization's Chairman Terry Duffy, it would set a $185 billion precedent. In other words, expect more MF Globals, beyond the CME's ability to backstop.

PFG Best repeated the MF Global scenario. The CFTC and other regulators checked out Peregrine Financial and found it in fine shape in January, 2012. The ensuing investigation found that the fraud extended back several years. It turned out that an account listed as holding $225 million only held $5 million. CEO and owner Russel Wassendorf attempted suicide over the debacle with a hose to the car. Thousands of clients lost money when their claims were illegally put behind the counter-claims of other banks. Again, JP Morgan is in the mix - this time holding the Forex transactions. Segregated accounts were raided, the funds 'vaporized.' Someone got them, of course. All customer accounts were frozen. People could not access their own positions, except some selling.

It's happened before. The National Futures Association signed off on audits of Sentinel Management Group a few weeks before the firm failed in 2007. As people's monies had been rehypothecated, Bank of NY Mellon filed suit for $312 million to be paid before depository clients. The suit was settled in August, 2012, in favor of BNYM. The clients lost. The suit sets a pretty frightening precedent - financial firms in bankruptcy can use client funds to pay off their debts. They can legally post client money as collateral and mingle client funds in emergency situations. Barnhardt posted a strident appeal to people to get over their "normalcy bias...get your money out now!"

High-Frequency Trading

In 2010, some of the most elite high-speed trading firms in the world began taking huge losses. These firms were started by PhD mathematicians, expert high-octane traders, and sophisticated financiers. They spent thousands of man-hours developing high-tech proprietary systems and tens of millions of dollars on the best equipment. They were shaving off milliseconds on trading. They were among the best in the business.

And they lost.

The savant Haim Bodek lost $300 million in the high frequency arena. There were hidden parties, some of the largest banks in the world, competing against him. They developed their own proprietary systems - ones that worked in a quasi-legal manner. They used some of the most elite high-frequency firms as 'insurance.' The favored tactic of the insiders was called the zero+ scalping strategy. The trader would never take a loss. Using a secret type of order, not a normal limit or market order, this order was designed after the system was reconfigured and only known to a few. Technically, anyone could use them, but most weren't aware of them. They allowed the traders to jump to the front of the queue with an invisible order, sitting and waiting.

In 2011, the SEC allowed certain traders to get better prices than the public through a new trading system. They allowed a rigged market to pass the rules. Public outcry made the company retract the system, but there is no way to know how many more systems exist without public knowledge.

The con-game isn't new. Professors Bill Christie and Paul Schultz proved in 1994 that floor traders - mainly the so-called market makers - were keeping spreads artificially wide. The 1/8 dollar minimum separation (this was before stocks traded in pennies) was only met 1% of the time. The typical spread was ¼ of a dollar - 25 cents. A spread is the difference between bid and ask. The spread is pocketed by the market makers. By doubling it, they doubled their profits at the expense of the average investor - mostly through mutual fund buying.

Mutual funds are the biggest chunk of dumb money out there. They buy millions of shares for middle class investors. These are the whales that get skimmed again and again and again.

They are very, very profitable when they're good. Getco, one of the larger HFT firms, went from $50 million a year in 2005 to $9 million a day in 2007. That money did not come from nowhere - it came from the 'dumb money.' And if you don't know who the dumb money is - that's not a good sign for your portfolio. There are hundreds of these firms skimming money off up and down markets. When the stock market lost 50% in 2008, Tactical Trading profited by $1 billion.

Since computer algorithms are running the trades, they have millions in place all the time. When big orders come in from mutual funds, representing the 'dumb' money, the con is triggered. As soon as the order comes in at a preset amount - say $65/share - the computer algorithm buys the stock at that price in front of the order that had the same price. It then sells the stock to the fund manager for a few cents more.

By being a preferred client for the stock exchanges, these high-frequency traders have many, many more trades - millions per day - than other traders. The exchange gives these traders special preference because they bring in so many fees. They receive queue priority. By being able to read market depth - the amount of buy and sell orders around the market price - the algos are able to execute trades so that they never take a loss. They constantly make tiny profits on millions of trades.

This zero+ strategy that ensures a loss never happens works in a brilliant manner. Because the computer knows there is an order at the same price behind it in the queue, it can flip the stock it just bought to the order behind it at the same price. No loss. By peering into market depth, the scalper can ensure he never takes a loss. That's the main game - zero loss. Then all the computers have to do is make millions of trades a day - the more trades, the more money. Even if 99% are scratches - 1% pay off. The machines never, ever lose money.

These hidden, elite teams put the other, very sophisticated traders, out of business.

In 2007, the uptick rule was removed. This rule forces short sellers to wait for an uptick in the price before selling short - it prevents a gaggle of shorts from plummeting a stock down in a frenzy. Without it, even a strong stock can be crushed in seconds, rendering huge losses to portfolios.

The daily number of trades on the market has increased by thousands of times. It's led to the flash crash phenomenon. The crash of 2:45 on May 6, 2010 dropped the Dow Jones by $600 in 3 minutes. It was a total drop of $1000 for the day, the largest in history. The market quickly recovered. The cause was HF trading. The traders accumulated a mere 200 contracts in the e-mini futures market, but traded an astounding 27,000. It was called a hot potato, as the algos swapped enormous positions back and forth. Some S&P 500 companies traded at one cent per share. Some companies went to $100,000 a share. Some traders put out stub orders – way out of the price range and not meant to be filled – with the intent of choking the system. This creates an imbalance in the orders, some quite delayed. The computers can see the orders before they hit on multiple exchanges. They try to manipulate an arbitrage (simultaneous price differential) between different exchanges. They also buy or short sell shares – frontrunning. If there's a big sell order, they short-sell ahead, driving down the price, then buy the shares back at the bottom of the sell limit. HFT trading was integral to the flash crash.

No one knows specifically why the flash crash happened or, more likely – those who know aren't telling. With these kinds of anomalies, somebody made a lot of money at somebody else's expense. Probably a number of market makers got creamed. At any rate, the event is clearly market manipulation, whether by accident or hidden design. It's another part of the shadow bank system and all the big banks are doing it.

Billionaire and hi-tech investor, Mark Cuban, calls HF traders the "ultimate hackers." They are trying to exploit the trading platforms, using software to outsmart software. It is a recipe for disaster. The argument that HFT narrows spreads and provides liquidity is absurd. The liquidity must already be there for HFT to function in a market. And bid spreads are meaningless to investors – they only matter for traders. To say this is a legitimate function is to say the stock market favors traders over investors.35 Indeed, one HF trader expressed serious concerns that algorithm terrorism could create global havoc.

It's a completely different stock market than it used to be. The stock market is totally rigged. Elite hidden players become very, very rich, by skimming billions away from ordinary investors every year. To emphasize the difference, in the 40s stocks were held for 4 years. 50 years later, that had dropped to 8 months as speculators dominated. 8 years later, it dropped to 2 months. Then the radical move to high-frequency trading happened starting in 2004. Now the average hold time is less than 20 seconds.

The ordinary investor cannot make money in this system. There are ways to avoid the high-frequency plague and still invest in equities. Mostly, you have to trade in thin markets. High-frequency traders need liquidity and lots of it. They need the money to flow like a river, so they can dip their buckets in over and over. A stock without a lot of orders is not a useful HFT target.

Unfortunately, it has a serious downside for the investor. Lack of liquidity creates a high spread - the difference between the bid (to buy) and the offer (to sell). To buy, you have to pay the spread. Example: bid is $5 and offer is $5.20. If you buy at the offer, your stock is immediately valued at the bid. You have lost 20 cents per share as soon as you purchase. That's why traders like liquid markets - the spread is usually only 1 cent.

The story of Knight Capital illustrates what can happen. Knight Capital was one of the most important brokers in several high-liquidity markets. They flash-crashed - lost everything. Their net worth ($600 million) disappeared in less than ten seconds. Their clients lost everything. That will be the trend from now on. The government and the banks have put in place multiple laws, regulations, and policies to confiscate customer funds from 'imploding' institutions.

They weren't even a company committing malfeasance. Nor were they even incompetent. They were probably very good at what they do. But they got stuck on the wrong end, caught in their own mechanism. They went down because their high-frequency trading system spiraled down an entire sector. That's the reality of the modern markets - no real stability can be found. All markets are unstable.

Knight's new trading platform was hacked - it seems. The platform went live a few days before it was meant to and began trading. It immediately vomited the company's capital, causing markets to go haywire. Lots of other investors were affected - a select few (that may have known ahead of time) made hundreds of millions of dollars. Many lost a lot of money.

The daily number of trades on the market has increased by thousands of times. It's led to the flash crash phenomenon. The crash of 2:45 on May 6, 2010 dropped the Dow Jones by $600 in 3 minutes. It was a total drop of $1000 for the day, the largest in history. The market quickly recovered. The cause was HF trading. The traders accumulated a mere 200 contracts in the e-mini futures market, but traded an astounding 27,000. It was called a hot potato, as the algos swapped enormous positions back and forth. Some S&P 500 companies traded at one cent per share. Some companies went to $100,000 a share. Some traders put out stub orders - way out of the price range and not meant to be filled - with the intent of choking the system. This creates an imbalance in the orders, some quite delayed. The computers can see the orders before they hit on multiple exchanges. They try to manipulate an arbitrage (simultaneous price differential) between different exchanges. They also buy or short sell shares - frontrunning. If there's a big sell order, they short-sell ahead, driving down the price, then buy the shares back at the bottom of the sell limit. HFT trading was integral to the flash crash.

No one knows specifically why the flash crash happened or, more likely - those who know aren't telling. With these kinds of anomalies, somebody made a lot of money at somebody else's expense. Probably a number of market makers got creamed. At any rate, the event is clearly market manipulation, whether by accident or hidden design. It's another part of the shadow bank system and all the big banks are doing it.

Billionaire and hi-tech investor, Mark Cuban, calls HF traders the "ultimate hackers." They are trying to exploit the trading platforms, using software to outsmart software. It is a recipe for disaster. The argument that HFT narrows spreads and provides liquidity is absurd. The liquidity must already be there for HFT to function in a market. And bid spreads are meaningless to investors - they only matter for traders. To say this is a legitimate function is to say the stock market favors traders over investors. Indeed, one HF trader expressed serious concerns that algorithm terrorism could create global havoc.

This does allow some opening for the everyday investor. The machines require a very tight spread - the difference between bid and ask prices. They need lots of liquidity - moving money - to utilize the algorithms. The average investor is strongly advised to stay out of highly liquid, big money markets - you will get slowly bled.

Smaller stocks, with larger bid-ask spreads, offer a safer place. The spread, unfortunately, costs you money the instant you buy - the stock is only worth the bid price, technically - because that's all you can get. But you must pay the ask price. A stock with a 5 cent or more spread is generally on the safe side. And that's not a big deal when the stock is $10 or more - unless you want to ditch it in less than a second. Then you would definitely lose - which is why the machines avoid these.

A couple of questions arise from this information. If the regulators take away HFT as a legal practice, will market liquidity dry up? It is claimed that the algos provide the massive market depth only available on the largest markets - the Dow, S&P, etc. Should we accept a less liquid market or accept a market run by pirates draining savers money and openly transferring enormous wealth from middle class to corporate predators?

Attorney General Eric Holder testified before House Appropriations Committee on April 4, 2012. Asked about HFT and his response to the problem, Holder said:

As I indicated in my opening statement, I've confirmed that the Department of Justice is looking at this matter, this subject area, as well. The concern is that people are getting an inappropriate advantage, information advantage, I guess competitive advantage, over others because of the way in which the system works. And apparently, as I understand it, and I'm just learning this, even milliseconds can matter, and so we're looking at this to try to determine if any federal laws, any Federal criminal laws, have been broken. This is also obviously something that the head of the SEC, Mary Jo White, would be looking at as well.

The central debate is that NYSE and the Nasdaq have permitted a split stock market. The common guy gets data from the SIP - it's slow and data is limited. The Direct Feed gives access to much faster and deeper data, but you can't have it. Only the wealthy Wall Street firms can. They get their better data ahead of your worse data. You lose. The Direct Feed holders buy your bid/offer instrument before you and sell/buy it with worse terms than you would have gotten otherwise. It doesn't seem like much until you realize that mutual fund managers are the prime targets. By buying large share blocks, they average out a much higher price than otherwise they would. The algos target their max price and force them to pay it for almost all of their large buys/sells.

Obviously, this relates to Financial Advisor problem. Financial Advisor are not really aware of this problem, or they don't care about it. Your portfolio suffers another of the death fo a thousand cuts.

Elizabeth Warren had more to say on HFT to the Senate on June 18, 2012.

For me the term high frequency trading seems wrong. You know this isn't trading. Traders have good days and bad days. Some days they make good trades and they make lots of money and some days they have bad trades and they lose a lot of money. But high frequency traders have only good days. In its recent IPO filing, the high frequency trading firm, Virtu, reported that it had been trading for 1,238 days and it had made money on 1,237 of those days...

High frequency trading reminds me a little of the scam in Office Space. You know, you take just a little bit of money from every trade in the hope that no one will complain. But taking a little bit of money from zillions of trades adds up to billions of dollars in profits for these high frequency traders and billions of dollars in losses for our retirement funds and our mutual funds and everybody else in the market place. It also means a tilt in the playing field for those who don't have the information or have the access to the speed or big enough to play in this game.

NYSE as well as Nasdaq are charged with maintaining fair and balanced markets - and get an F. The SIP/Direct Feed creates a dual market - one for most people and one for the big money traders. This big money is siphoning your money away. Make no mistake. Where else can the money come from? It also pays up to half a billion a year for the privilege of the fast, full data. They also offer 'colocation' meaning that these players sit as close as possible - in the same building- in order to get the data and the orders moved faster and faster.

New York's Attorney General has begun an investigation into the legality of this situation. By the interpretation of Mercer Bullard, lawyer and former SEC counsel, it is insider trading.

Bullard said: "In a market dominated by electronic trading, investors are having their pockets picked — and individual investors and mutual fund shareholders are among the likely victims. The securities exchanges' practice of selling early access to their trading data to insiders — as the term 'insiders' suggests — is a practice that looks like illegal insider trading."

Bullard says the requirement that insider traders have to be trading on material, i.e., very important non-public information, is met by the fact that if it wasn't important information, the insiders with the Direct feeds couldn't be reaping "huge profits" on it.

Investors only have one source of profit - other investors. But they have two sources of losses - other investors and traders. The money flows in one direction. Traders call investors 'dumb money.' It moves slowly. Fast money, the smart money, always beats the slow money, the dumb money. And I have to be brutally honest here - any financial adviser is dumb money. And he's using your money to be dumb money.

Fraudster stories

Kerry Scharfenberger was arrested for fraud in Alberta in 2012. He made off with $400k in investor funds while working for Investors Group. Even the largest companies are not immune to their advisers committing fraud. It is absolutely rampant. The system actually encourages it and many, many advisers get away with it. Many are never caught. Most are caught only because they lose ALL their clients' money. As long as they only lose a percentage of the money, they can usually continue in perpetuity - or at least until they lose all their clients.

Scammers are hard to spot. Typically, they possess the proper training to come off professionally. They are quite skilled at their trade - liberating you from your money. They often do extensive preparatory work by getting involved in trade groups, joining civic organizations to develop authenticity and trust, attaining like-minded attittudes with potential victims, seeking targets in tightly knit organizations which foster trust - especially churches, senior groups, golf clubs and restricted organizations. They often give money to charity. Using these activities, they will spread their network through the 'clients' network. Using their charitable involvement, they gain promotion from prominent community members.

Only the most egregious get caught. If they are truly clever at cycling the money through other contacts and businesses and if they don't take too much, it can be almost impossible to prove the theft. But it happens to thousands of people every day. Frequently they get power of attorney over client funds - this is tantamount to simply giving them the money outright.

Often, the perps display strong tendencies of psychopathology - shown in several studies. They do not care about others opinions or feelings, but are terribly charismatic and bright. They excel at deceit, trickery, and have a penchant for dangerous hobbies.

The 'financial psychopath' seems to be a great leader, a wonderful employee or prospective one, a great team player and a friend since the tendencies they have exist unseen behind their façade. They do great in a high-stress, exciting workplace and can manipulate corporate structures and methods. Within this, they tend to take advantage of poor communications and create divisions between people for their own utility.

Unfortunately—writes the author—the best candidates for many Wall Street jobs exhibit the traits of a financial psychopath. Even Bloomberg noted that the financial crisis was caused by 'corporate psychopaths.'

Psychologist and business ethicist Clive Boddy wrote, They are "extraordinarily cold, much more calculating and ruthless towards others than most people are and therefore a menace to the companies they work for and to society. They cheerfully lie about their involvement in events, are very convincing in blaming others for what has happened and have no doubts about their own worth and value. They are happy to walk away from the economic disaster that they have managed to bring about, with huge payoffs and with new roles advising governments how to prevent such economic disasters."

"At one major investment bank for which I worked," a senior exec from a large UK bank confessed, "we used psychometric testing to recruit social psychopaths because their characteristics exactly suited them to senior corporate finance roles." The bank actively sought out psychopaths because it made them more 'successful!'

The lawyer tasked with investigating Lehman's collapse found a culture of risk-taking and psychopathic behavior. And that seems to be the norm across businesses. High performers, like Sir Fred Godwin of RBS, are praised effusively - until they are found to have caused massive losses by risk - $24 billion in Godwin's case. The man took down one of the largest banks in Britain, causing massive pain for investors in the process. He was considered a hero. That's the state of play in financial services today. (These traits also appear in very high percentages among politicians, by the way). Even the former chief economist for the IMF, Simon Johnson, warns that a 'quiet coup' has taken place. Now our governments are owned by the financial sector.

The take-away? Those responsible for the 2008 crisis are still in power. They feel zero remorse or regret over the actions to cause that. In fact, they have gotten sickeningly rich by destroying the economy. And they are still going strong. Make no mistake - you are in the line of fire if you allow this system to manage any of you savings. Boddy warns that they are now advising governments how to deal with the crisis - giving them strategies to steal the wealth of most of the world.

The preceding shows just how systemic the fraud is - it is institutionalized at the top. That's why there were no convictions from the 2008 crisis. The investigators were hamstrung by the politicians. But this story extends to the trenches - to your neighborhood licensed financial advisor. There are too many fraud stories of financial advisers to even begin, but here is a sampling of some just for an idea.

Thieving Minister

Stefan Wilson' Ponzi scam wrecked the finances of dozens of families. He sold people an 20%+ rate of return and delivered it for a few years based on new investors. These were not rich people and they lost everything. He told them to hock their house because the returns too good to pass up. They wound up homeless, many old ladies. It's important to realize that these people had great trust in Wilson - he was a church minister and a very charming, engaging man. Most financial advisers running scams are very agreeable people. Wilson's organization used the principal invested to pay out returns. All the investments lost money.

Among his victims were a disabled vet and an elderly couple who lost their farm and multi-generational home.

Pet Fraud

Eric Stein pulled in $49 million. He had nearly 2000 victims. The scam? Return a Pet franchises. These cost up to 50 grand - they issued tags to help lost pets get home. But the business was a giant fraud, using paid endorsements and other deceptions.

Charity Fraud

New Era lured initial investors to pony up $5000, then doubled it (from another business) in a few months. Then it ramped up into a more or less garden variety Ponzi, pulling in new investors to pay off the senior investors. After a high-profile charity received a donation from the money made, a slew of charities jumped on the bandwagon. It's notable that these were paid financial professionals who directed their charities to invest a total of $350+ millions. Even the wealthy fell for it, and they usually receive much better advice than the middle class (Bernie Madoff's fund took over $50 billion - this wasn't the average investor - it was old money.) Everybody can fall for this and nobody believes they are at the time.

Spring Harbor College had a prof who started speaking about his concerns over New Era. The admin wouldn't listen and kept its money in the organization.

Frankel Case

Martin Frankel purchased insurance companies and pilfered them. Investors lost several hundred million dollars from his various companies. Frankel had no lows, setting up the St. Francis of Assisi fund to deliberately defraud investors and using it as cover from the SEC, since he was barred from trading.

Cybertech

Cybernet seemed to be the up and coming internet company that would rival IBM. Everyone was fooled, even very sophisticated investment agencies. It turned out that a cabal of extremely sophisticated white-collar criminals created a company, then pulled in investors by the thousands using fake offices and tricky accounting. It was an enormous machine for theft and fraud.

Ringleader Barton Watson and his team, generated a huge conspiracy of fraudulent collateral, income tax records, accounts payables, and finance records to garner loans and other bank products far in excess of the company's value - since it really had none. They got additional and larger loans to repay previous loans and to live the high life.

Many financial instituions were defrauded. The most notable take-away is clear - if banks, who have the highest bar for preventing such fraud - can be victimized - what chance do you have?

This system will bleed you dry - if you're lucky. Or it will rob everything outright, if you're not.

Watson killed himself when the FBI came for him.

TYCO

The CEO of Tyco, Dennis Kzlowski, claimed he had the right to take and use company money for what he did. He spent millions on a birthday party for his wife. TYCO bought him a $30 million apartment. His claim to innocence? He did it openly. Any jury would convict him despite his right to use the money that way.

He may be right about being innocent of a crime. That's the startling fact. Many corporate CEO's live extremely lavish lifestyles - paid for by the company, of course. They simply mandate a huge pay increase for themselves and their cronies. And that brings up a very critical question: Is it prudent to invest in a company that has about a 50/50 chance of being led by a pseudo-criminal, one who uses the law to steal? Because that's exactly where your financial adviser has you invested right now.

First International Bank

A small group of cons passed themselves off as finance geniuses and ripped off 3000+ investors to the tune of $175 mil. Their front was Grenada. The group drove numerous people into bankruptcy and shattered old age finances.

The take-away? Even if some of the money is recovered - it goes to Uncle Sam. The victims do not get any back in most cases unless the thieves are solvent.

Christie's Auction house and Sotheby's Auction house

The two most venerable auction houses on Earth are Christie's and Sotheby's. In the 2000's bother were convicted of price-fixing collusion. Some of the wealthiest people in the US were victims. It came from a problem - they were competing so fiercely that they nearly dropped their commissions to nothing. So to fix it, they fixed the game. $250 million was paid in restitution after a civil case.

It's alarming to see that even the most venerable and trusted firms, in the world of fine arts and collectibles, are completely corrupt. The message is stark - it's very difficult to trust even very reputable organizations.

Baptist Foundation

Continuing the Christian theme of using God for graft, the Baptist Foundation of Arizona stole the life savings from several thousand older couples - destroying their retirement. BFA used a couple of satellite orgs - New Church Ventures and ALO - to funnel money and make the books look 'right.' The real estate investments were crap, plain and simple.

ALO 'bought' bad real estate from BFA with New Church as the financier. These financed purchases were listed on the BFA books as assets. At disclosure, ALO's balance sheet was red to $175 million. New Church had a bevy of worthless notes it held for BFA. When the scheme collapsed, many innocent lives were destroyed. It's sad, but your church could be the most dangerous place to look for investment advice. There may be a shark in the water. That's because a recommendation within a church or using the services of a church member carries an automatically higher badge of trust. But that trust is often misplaced.

Accounts and Fraud

The most trusted name in accounting was once Arthur Anderson. They signed off on BFA's statements. However, they didn't use GAAP - Generally Accepted Accounting Principles. They were committing fraud. Notice that the best name firms in the world were involved in fraud. That's the standard now - Arthur Anderson also helped Enron.

Accountants need to pay much better attention to potential fraud when doing external audits. As Enron proved, even a venerable firm such as Arthur Anderson can go to the dogs with a mere change in management. When a charismatic crook sits in the head office, the company will post deceptive financial reports and sucker unsuspecting investors. Use of external audits, doctored to look good, is a classic technique. It's being used by many, many firms today. In fact, an executive order from 2008 specifically allows large banks to ignore proper accounting standards. If the truth was known, they say, it would be a national security concern! That's pretty troubling.

If the government is concerned enough over national security in light of a major bank's balance sheet, then it must be pretty bad. Let's be honest - the Federal government has given the major banks carte blanche to commit financial fraud with Presidential backing.

NSYNC Manager robs investors blind

The manager of the Back Street Boys and NSync - Lou Pearlman - pulled in tons of investors using that success and robbed them. People were fooled. He should be trustworthy because he's successful. But he was a crook. It's the usual story, too - retirees, pensioners and even sophisticated investors - Pearlman even robbed his friends. And he already had a lot of money.

Health Care Fraud

Richard Scrushy started HealthSouth - it put rehabilitative services into clinics instead of hospitals. A great idea, it actually made a ton of money legitimately. Scrushy was incredibly charming and winning in public, but inside the business, he was almost demonic. He also engaged in big money securities fraud. After the initial success, the company tapered off. Scrushy wanted to please 'the Street,' so he ordered the CFO to cook the books. Fearfully, he complied. The deception grew and grew, until the CFO ran to the regulators and turned over the whole deal - a lie to the tune of $2 and half billion.

Economan

Al Parish had a great reputation locally as an investing genious. A local newsguy and a trusted citizen of Charleston. He got very rich very quick. His customers are raking in 30% returns and bragging. He has 612 investors at a high point. But the SEC spots a small anomaly.

It snowballs into a full on investigation by outraged people. His program - $130 million - was a classic Ponzi. Investors got bilked, again. Don't be those people.

Fire your financial adviser or investment guru. Take charge of your own finances. It's not that hard.

How to slowly lose - Modern Portfolio Theory

I quit being a Financial Advisor. In order to make money, you have to put your clients money at risk - Joe S. former financial advisor

One of the big deceptions of Modern Portfolio Theory (which your advisor will probably steer you towards) is called diversification. Warren Buffet famously called it di-worse-ification. The idea is that diversification protects against market downturns. This is true, but it only protects against sector downturns, not general market downturns. In 2008, diversified investors were creamed- it made no difference, or made it worse.

The following chart shows the ROI of investors versus other types of investment by businesses. The best a diversified investor can hope for, on average, is about 11%. That's actually considered a pretty good return. When you consider that Walter Jon Williams calculated true inflation at near 10%, that's a pretty minimal return. And factoring in the current distortions in the currency, Treasury situation, and interest rates, returns for anyone diversified into bonds will be considerably worse. Interest rates are extremely low, artificially held down. This kills returns for the most conservative investor. Risk-free returns on 10 year bonds are below 2%.

Risk-free is a big lie, anyway. Sure, if you wait until maturity (10 long years) you will get your 2%, but this is well below true inflation. It's even below the government's rigged numbers. (I cover this in detail in my other book Gold Wars). By investing in Treasuries, you are actually losing wealth, even though the nominal return is positive. Further, the dollar is in jeopardy. It is looking likely to suffer a serious devaluation due to debt stresses and foreign creditor fatigue. It's mathematically inevitable and the end will be sooner rather than later.

There is an even uglier side to Treasuries, however. If the interest rates go up, then existing Treasuries at the lower rates lose value VERY rapidly. No one wants a 2% Treasury when a 3 or 4% Treasury is ready to buy. And if rates go to where they should be - north of 6% considering US finances - they're all but worthless. Those high rates also lead to high printing to cover the interest, leading to devaluation of the currency, leading to a lower value for existing Treasuries, leading to the need for more and more Treasuries, leading to a spiral downward.

This is exacerbated by the enormous load of existing Treasuries. When the game rolls over, holders will start to dump them. This could lead to a panic, where Treasuries go no-bid. No one will buy them at any price. Admittedly, this is highly unlikely - the Fed will continue to be the buyer of last resort. But this leads to an out of control monetary printing cycle. There is no escape - the US dollar will decline steeply and soon after, the Treasuries will lose value and interest rates will rise. Either that, or the Fed will buy all the new and old Treasuries on the market and the currency will go through a massive inflation, possibly a hyperinflation.

US dollar denominated bonds - corporate or government - are not a good investment.

And that goes double, triple for muni bonds. The big banks have sold the munis down the river. Their bonds are a hot mess - due for serious drawdowns without any Federal help all over the country. If your FA has you in muni bonds, then you should fire him before reading another word. If he has you in Treasuries (and he probably does have some) have him answer some pointed questions:

1) Are Treasuries going lower? Current holdings will gain value if they do and fall if they rise. Short-term Treasuries are already negative, or near so. There is no downward room. If you have a lot of capital (over $250k) then it's not unreasonable to park some in 3 month Treasuries. This protects you from an FDIC style failure where your excess capital is 'vaporized.' But this is the only reasonable situation for this.

2) Should I be worried about the huge amount of US debt before investing in Treasuries?

3) What rate do Interest Rate Swaps play in the Treasury market? He will not know what you're talking about - I almost guarantee it. Interest rate swaps are a market, primarily around US Treasuries, that 'insure' against a sizeable change in the return rate. IRS's are being used to leverage additional purchases of Treasuries in a very convoluted system. See this article by Rob Kirby for a detailed, if challenging, explanation of this very complex system. One very good rule of investing - do not play in markets you do not understand. And the Treasury market is very, very complicated. It seems straightforward enough to the average investor. It is not. It is a death-trap for the unsophisticated.

4) What are the Chinese doing in regards to their enormous Treasury holdings and how will it affect my portfolio? He will hem and haw, and probably state that the

Chinese need to keep the US as a trade partner to ensure they have someone to sell their goods to. This is a big lie. Why on earth would the Chinese need to exchange valuable labor and goods for a pile of paper they can never spend that is constantly losing value? The only reason is to maintain high employment and prevent civil unrest. But they can simply throw the goods in the river and pay people for making them - that's the magic of fiat.

The Chinese are steadily disposing of their Treasuries and masking that action to prevent a bond panic so their holdings maintain value. They claim to have $3.8 trillion. However, China has a history of 'sudden' revisions of reserves numbers. Their gold reserves tripled overnight in the mid-2000's when they announced a secret accumulation for several years prior to that. China is using those reserve assets to buy up enormous amounts of land, ports in commercial cities, a massive equity portfolio, large resources in Africa and the Mid-East, and lots and lots of GOLD. The Chinese leaders are keeping it secret, but eventually, it will be revealed. At that time, if you are on the 'wrong side of the trade' you will be hit very, very hard.

At any rate, bonds are supposed to be a very smart, conservative way to diversify. I would never recommend bonds to my clients in the current environment - the risks are higher than people realize and the rewards are negligible. Your FA will no doubt highly recommend a portion of your portfolio in bonds. This should be a cause for concern.

Diversification is also meant to spread your money throughout multiple sectors to prevent serious losses in the event 'tech' or 'retail' take a nosedive. But just as it limits losses in sector downturns, it sharply limits profits from sector upturns. If only a small part of your portfolio rides the wave, then you get a smaller profit.

Most financial advisors will try to diversify you. They aren't helping you out at all. As Warren Buffet called this Modern Portfolio Theory trap - Diworsification. Diversification within stocks harms your portfolio. But what does that mean? I'll let the good folks at Investopedia help out here.

Diversification Beyond Stocks
Investopedia Staff on January 25, 2014
One thing even the newest investor understands, or has at least heard of, about a portfolio is diversification - blending a variety of asset classes to reduce exposure to risk. But a well-diversified stock portfolio is just one component of putting together the best possible portfolio.

Diversifying not just among different stocks, but among different assets, is how an investor can truly mitigate risk. Even with a well-diversified stock portfolio, an individual is still exposed to market risk (or systematic risk as finance professors like to call it), which cannot be diversified away by adding additional stocks.

What Exactly Is Diversification?
Basically, diversification among asset classes works by spreading your investments among various assets (e.g. stocks, bonds, cash, T-bills, real estate, etc.) with low correlation to each other. This allows you to reduce volatility in your portfolio, because different assets move up and down in price at different times and at different rates. Thus, having a portfolio diversified among different assets creates more consistency and improves overall portfolio performance.

How Does Correlation Work?
Correlation is simple: If two asset classes are perfectly correlated, they are said to have a correlation of +1. This

means that they move in lockstep with each other, either up or down. A completely random correlation - a relationship in which one asset's chance of going up is equal to the chance of dropping if the other asset rises or falls - is said to be a correlation of 0. Finally, if two asset classes move in exact opposition - for every upward movement of one there is an equal and opposite downward movement of another, and vice versa - they are said to be perfectly negatively correlated, or have a correlation of -1.

A Diversified Stock Portfolio vs. a Diversified Portfolio of Assets

When we talk about diversification in a stock portfolio, we're referring to an investor's attempt to reduce exposure to unsystematic risk (i.e. company-specific risk) by investing in various companies across different sectors, industries or even countries.

When we discuss diversification among asset classes, the same concept applies, but over a broader range. By diversifying among different asset classes, you are reducing the risk of being exposed to the systemic risk of any one asset class.

Like holding one company in your stock portfolio, having your entire net worth in a portfolio of any one asset - even if that portfolio is diversified - constitutes the proverbial "all of your eggs in one basket." Despite the mitigation of unsystematic risk (risk associated with any individual stock), you are still very much exposed to market risk. By investing in a number of different assets, you reduce this exposure to market risk or the systemic risk of any one asset class.

The basic problem is that diversification within the stock market gives you some downside protection against a particular stock failing, but it gives you no upside juice. Moreover, it gives you zero protection against global market crashes. All the boats fall together. Thing is, when your broker wants to diversify you, he wants you to own a bunch of different stocks - not a variety of non-stock assets - except bonds. He won't put you in real estate - it doesn't pay his mortgage. He won't put in precious metals for the same reason. He may be forbidden by the terms of his license to recommend gold or silver, anyway. And that's a huge disservice to you.

Modern Portfolio Theory requires - by regulation - that a fund be like its reference index - say the DOW or the Russell mid-cap index. When the fund manager outperforms the index by a decent margin - 12% instead of 8% - it is assumed by industry standards to happen because of increased risk. Money managers are required to take client moneys out of such funds due to the industry assumption of increased risk for that enhanced reward. These investors wanted lower risk. A fund manager can get better returns, but by doing so, he jeopardizes the amount of assets under holdings. He is punished for gaining superior returns! By managing a better fund, he actually makes less money. The market is structured to use Modern Portfolio Theory in this way - by the regulators - to flatten investor returns. Those increased returns are called 'volatility.' MPT assumes that increased returns and hence volatility equals increased risk - a patent falsehood. Risk is the most poorly measured and evaluated aspect of Financial Advisors. They don't get it and it is misrepresented to the middle class.

Fund managers know this, although FA's may not. However, they keep this info very close in the pocket. It's quite damaging. If you're a fund manager and you know that you are relegated to underperform the market, you want it kept in the closet. It would destroy the mutual fund industry if this were general knowledge. Yet this is the bane of the terrible Modern Portfolio Theory - it causes deep damage to your financial interests. And every FA is more or less required to abide by it, especially if their clients choose so-called 'low-risk' investments.

Fund managers must adhere closely to the benchmark or they lose deep pocket 'clients' in the form of money managers. Obviously, when the fees are factored into this equation - it is guaranteed that the client will do worse than the index fund itself. The best fund managers are totally locked in by this system. They cannot do better by their clients. This is the regulatory structure which will punish you. It's not even your FA's fault. It's systemic, as most of these problems are. You are FAR better off managing your own money and putting it in an index, especially suing a collar (described in the ignorance of good investment strategies section). A collar can drastically limit your losses without any cost to you. These protective structures are easy to do and take only a few minutes per week. Your FA will not, indeed probably cannot, set one up for you. The regulations of his trade prohibit it.

Ignoring the Crisis

This is one of my favorite 'sins' of FA's - simply pretending everything is fine. It is not fine. The list of economic and financial problems is very, very long. If you begin discussing them, you will most likely be called a 'doom and gloomer,' as if periodic economic resets were mythical like gnomes. It's bizarre, the Pollyanna lie which decimates investors. Many people were poo-pooed in early 2008 for their concerns. IF they listened to themselves and protected their assets in one way or another - they mostly did okay. But most listened to their brokers and suffered major drawdowns. Some were wiped out.

Now they are singing the same song of the Goldilocks economy. The song was a lie before;w why would it be true now? Ask your broker if he is concerned about any of the following and how he sees the outcome of these situations:

- Monstrous US debt
- Demise of most fiat currencies
- Unprecedented QE
- Shadow Banking System deleveraging
- Derivatives risk
- Trade war/currency war
- China Russia, et al standoff against the West
- Institutionalized graft by the big banks (if he denies this, point to HSBC laundering money, the LIBOR fixing scandal, the mortgage scandals, robo-signing, gold-price fixing, the London Whale, and a host of others.
- Manipulation of the major US indexes by the President's working group on markets.
- Lunatic P/E ratios on some of the hottest companies
- Manipulated stats on inflation to make GDP look good, validate more printing, and keep Social Security payments low (among other things).
- Destruction of capital by Zero Interest Rate Policy (he won't have a clue what you mean).

Ask him what gold miner he recommends. It will be a major. IF he says Newmont, that's okay. If he says Barrick - run like hell- he's a fool. Ask him about silver and its relation to gold as a bulwark in your portfolio. Tell him you want some exposure to PM's. If he recommends GLD or SLV, RUN while firing him over your shoulder.

Stuck in Mutual Fund Purgatory

In 2012, the S&P 500 roared up 16% including dividends. During that period, less than 40% of fund managers beat the market. Most investors could have simply invested in an index fund, paid less in fees, and done better. 60% of investors did worse with a financial adviser than without one just by owning the S&P or Dow. If you spread out performance over two years (2011 and 2012) the results are even worsen with only 10% of funds beating the market. If we stretch back even further, the results are even more dismal. For the ten years ended 1Q 2013, a mere 0.4% of mutual funds have beaten the market. And guess what? Your genius FA will almost undoubtedly put you in mutual funds.

These fund managers are investment "professionals," folks whose jobs depend on producing gains, who cannot beat the market for any significant period. The reason this fact is not better known is because the mutual fund industry usually closes its losing funds or merges them with other, better performing funds. As a result, the mutual fund industry in general experiences a tremendous survivor bias. But the cold hard fact what I told you earlier: less than half of one percent of fund managers outperform the market over a ten-year period. Why?

The market is rigged in multiple ways against the average investor or financial advisor. If you're not institutional money, then you are meat. It's that simple. HFT trading skims profits on millions of transactions. Most of these are mutual fund managers - the so-called dumb money - taking their big, slow positions. The PPT prevents the market from falling below certain levels and gooses rises from time to time. This creates an artificial market separated from Main Street reality, a crisis awaiting discovery - at your expense. Dark pools – invisible exchanges of stocks – trade massive shares off the normal, transparent markets. All of these activities occur without general public knowledge. Short of an open knowledge of critical market operations, the average investor cannot win.

The titanic skimming operation is officially sanctioned, but the means are not available to most investors. Eventually the system will crash. When HFT trading hits a big momentum play to the downside, it will accelerate the momentum – that's how it functions. The Fed will be unable to buy in to stop the massive selling. Its pool will be overwhelmed. And your mutual fund will suffer catastrophic losses.

Mutual fund managers also fail to anticipate, understand, or properly respond to the business cycle. This cycle is one of rises and falls, but in recent decades, these have exacerbated into booms and busts - courtesy of the Federal Reserve. The Fed overprints causing a boom. This leads to malinvestment - think dotcom bubble after Greenspan printed up a storm, or weird real estate vehicles from the mid-2000's. Inevitably, the bubble (or bubbles) pops and the market sector tanks. As a side note, we're currently headed for a general market collapse because the bubble is pervasive.

The fund manager is ignorant of these dynamics. He understands a business cycle well enough, but has little idea that it is driven in wider and more rapid swings by Central Bank actions. His mandate is to remain totally invested, too, so he will not suddenly pull out of the market based on belief in a coming crash. He most likely will never see the signs. And that's pretty bad news for investors.

There are a host of reasons why the mutual fund market and the entire system is essentially a wealth transfer mechanism from the middle class to connected insiders. Basically, the standard investment strategy for the middle class is death by a thousand cuts. That is how Financial Advisers are trained to invest you. They are trained by a system that views you as a cow to be milked for steady profits. When you really get this, you will never use a financial adviser again.

Another ugly scam is the B-Shares fund. These are pretty much gone, without explanation, but they're bad. A B-Share, which many, many advisors used for clients, forced an investor to pay a 'surrender charge' and quite a high one, to liquidate their shares early - before 7 years, usually. If your fund tanks, you get to pay even more on top of your losses to get out of a bad investment. And most FA's that put their clients in these more awful than standard awful funds never warned their clients about the problem of having their money trapped for years.

In one story, the advisor outright lied to their client about an annuity fund. He claimed they could walk away without penalty, but it was not true. They would have lost all their interest - $7000. They had to hold the instrument for another 4 years. This is still very common - trapping the money. It's especially odious in today's market with pathetic, artificial interest rates. Your money can be trapped at below inflation interest (guaranteed unless the entity goes bankrupt) for years. And if rates rise like they really, really should? You lose even worse. And if the currency gets devalued by the necessities of debt overhang or printing induced inflation or sovereign attack or Petrodollar demise or...? You lose big and you can't do anything about it - your advisor has trapped your money for his commission - one that he gets again each year by trapping your money in these cages.

Ignorance of good investment strategies

In 2006, the CEO of a major financial firm invested a large chunk of money in Ford motor company. When questioned about the decision, he said, "Boy, do they know how to make a car." He risked client money on the vague proposition that they can make a car and therefore the stock would rise. Needless to say, that is a necessary criteria, but it is hardly sufficient for such a judgment. More information is clearly needed. The most important question

- Is Ford undervalued or overvalued - was ignored. This was the CEO of a financial firm - a top professional in the field! This should show you the state of play of many financial analysts. They're a long way below the CEO, who presumably got there for some reason. And if the CEO says 'buy' the field workers buy. With your money.

But it's much worse than this simple story shows. There are a myriad of beneficial ways to 'invest' with very limited risk. Options and futures are the best among them. Options original use was to limit risk with stocks - and properly used, they can do this very, very well. One very conservative technique is called a collar - and it can be implemented at no cost, or even a slight credit. You simply buy a put and sell a call on stock that you already own. The call should be above the price of the stock and the put below. The proceeds from the call pay for the put. On major stocks, you can do this each week to keep the 'insurance' in line with the instrument's price.

If the stock rises past the call price, your stock will be 'called away' at a profit. You can simply buy it back and repeat the process. If your stock falls below the put price, you will assign it at the put price, thus limiting your loss. Typical ranges are 2-5% wide of the current stock price when setting the collar up. This allows you a gain of that much, while limiting your loss to the same. This is a good, conservative way to play a steadily rising stock. In the event of a market crash - you are safe.

However, no advisor will ever set this extremely sensible protection up for you. Why not? First, it's a lot of hassle for no money. Second, they're not allowed to buy and sell options. In other words - the system prevents your advisor from giving you one of the best tools for financial protection. It's rigged against you. I can do this (and I do) and I'm not a financial advisor. I won't be one because it limits what you can do for your clients. As one fellow who quit the job said - 'Being a financial advisor requires you to put your clients' money at risk.' Read that again - it's the basis of this whole book. All financial advisors, by the certification they hold, are required to put your money on the block and cannot keep it as safe as you can by yourself with some very simple tools. And they don't want to take the time to do it, anyway.

- Brokers do not understand options or how they can be used to protect your portfolio.
- They know nothing about particular sectors.
- They only invest you (most) in mutual or index funds.
- They will never recommend precious metals because they usually don't understand/see the current problems in the monetary system. (They only see the debt issues).
- They are not allowed to recommend Gold as an investment - their license (in most cases) prohibits it. They make no money off of your buying it anyway.

According to the records, 75% of fund managers did worse than the S&P - losing almost 1% per year compared to their benchmark - compounded, of course. During a 25 year period ending in early 2000's, the index (S&P) returned 12.3% per year. The mutual fund mean return was 10.3%, but the investors in those funds saw a pathetic 7.3% per year - barely 60% of the index return. A handful of funds (1 in 25) beat the index, but only by a skinny 0.6%. The majority got their asses handed to them with a 5% underperformance. The smart money refers to mutual funds as 'dumb money.' They are not wrong.

Market questions you MUST ask your Financial Advisor
Why are bonds so low?
What's the deal with Goldman Sachs?
Are the big banks in trouble?

What is an interest rate swap?

Should I invest in real estate/local business/gold/ (or anything that does not give the FA a profit)? Why not? Is it because you only make money when I invest the way you want?

How is money created?

Is the Petrodollar standard real?

What is it?

What are the consequences of it failing?

The long version of this is available in my other book Gold Wars: The Battle for the Global Economy, but the brief version starts with debt. Bonds are low because the Federal Reserve is monetizing the national debt - outright buying Treasuries for cash they print. They have to keep the interest rate low or the interest burden will collapse the whole scheme. They also have to protect certain banks/financial companies. Goldman Sachs is one of these and the company has deep tentacles in the various departments - several of the last heads of the Treasury, the Federal Reserve and the NY Fed (the real one) have been GS employees. Goldman Sachs, working with JP Morgan and Citigroup, dictate currency policy and debt policy. They do not do so to serve the public - you are not invited to the feast. You are the indentured servant not getting paid.

In fact, during the 2008 crisis, only one company was paid out 100 cents on the dollar for derivative bets - Goldman Sachs.

Banking Sector Problems

When it changes it does so quickly, and the impossible becomes the inevitable without ever having been probable ~ Bill Fleckenstein, Fleckenstein Capital

Has your advisor warned you about bail-ins? Ask him if he knows what they are. The Cyprus flame-out with its main bank set the stage and the G-20 meeting in late 2014 made it official: legalized bail-ins are now policy. A bail-in means that your bank account can be used to fund your bank if it finds itself in serious financial trouble. And most big banks are candidates for that. Depositor money has now become merely an unsecured credit owed to you by your bank. In the event of the bank have a financial catastrophe, deposits above a certain threshold (depends on the region and other factors) can be defaulted on, or more likely, exchanged for bank stock. The stocks will almost immediately drop in value because a bank that does this will be publicly proclaiming its own insolvency and diluting shares massively at the same time. It will also signal to future clients to STAY AWAY - bad bank in big trouble. Such a bank will get a balance sheet bump and face a steady, steep decline into bankruptcy.

That's after even the gimme the banks get. The Fed is loaning the banks money at a paltry 0.25% interest rate. They then turn around and buy short-term bonds from the Treasury for 0.5% interest. It's a guaranteed profit at government (taxpayer) expense! But it still begs the question why rates are so low? There's a number of reasons, but it's clear any rate increase would crush the mega-banks, flip over the 'bond carry trade' and ram up rates by at least 2%. With the volume of the outstanding debt, that would kill the banks. Why? They have a combined total of $330 trillion in interest rate swaps. You read that right - $300,000 billion. The banks net worth is about $6 trillion. 50 to 1 - now that's leverage. The banks should be popped like a bad blister on society's ass.

The JPM depositary funds hit $1.34 trillion November, 2014 - still going up. Their loan portfolio maxed in 2008 at $761 billion, then kept going down. The banks are not loaning the bailout money to Main Street, despite having more than enough depositor backing to make loans. They are running the above described 'carry trade', a softball profit pitch thrown by the FED, for massive profits. The CB's are floating the banks - and you're paying the bill without ever seeing it.

This bleeds into the markets in a bad way. Seeking returns in a ZIRP (zero interest rate policy) environment pushes investors into risk in the markets. This is a prelude to another financial crisis stemming from exuberance and imbalanced capital markets.

Global markets are hideously risky and completely interconnected. It may be impossible to really know what's going on at a global level, even given far more information than we have. Large banks in every country, central banks and even governments are notoriously secretive about their financial practices, and if secrecy doesn't pose enough difficulties for getting a grip on the situation, then there's the rampant lying and fraud. Banks have off-balance sheet transactions to hide their real bets. Governments do, too. Federal liabilities are estimated at $60 to $100 trillion by credible estimates, when Medicare and other programs are included. The largely off-balance derivatives complex is between $600 and $1400 trillion. It's the world's largest economic unknown, a mushroom cloud waiting to blow up the global economy. When it goes off in a chain reaction, the world's biggest institutions will become black holes, sucking in more and more money to stay alive. I recommend removing all funds from the major banks - JP Morgan, Citibank, Bank of America, HSBC and so forth. Put it in a local bank or credit union. This supports your own community and keeps your money safer and the holders more accountable.

The Dodd-Frank Act was supposed to regulate derivatives, getting them out into the open, where problems would be easier to anticipate and solve. But it does something pretty frightening, as well – it ostensibly backstops the massive derivatives complex. Dodd-Frank opens a Fed borrowing line to derivatives clearing-houses that are found to be 'systemically important.' This is the essence of moral hazard. No one has had access to this channel of cheap money before except savings banks, which are regulated in their use. The clearing-houses are not regulated. They can do anything they want with the money they borrow at ultra-low rates. If they get into a serious derivatives rats-nest, they borrow money for nothing, and never pay it back. It's all reward and no risk. Again, bet the farm and bet big. Become systemically important by taking the counter-bets to the biggest institutions. If the clearing-houses go bust, those institutions go bust, too. Now, they're systemically important. If their bets win, they win. If their bets lose, the Fed pays off. There is no reason not to bet the farm, because they can't really lose.

The 2005 bankruptcy law subordinated bank held assets to derivatives. In English, that means you can lose ALL YOUR MONEY in one swoop. It's already happened to some people. Let me explain. The law states that when a financial firm goes bankrupt, the first to be paid are not the standard creditors, but those with counterparty derivatives - gambling debts. Derivatives, of course, are HUGE - in excess of a quadrillion dollars. That's many times the size of the global economy and over 1000 times the US asset base! It's thermonuclear financial practice.

And to make it worse, your stocks, your bonds, anything any investment company 'holds' for you is legally their property, not yours. You only hold a claim to it. When the fan gets struck by the defecation, your claim will go up in smoke. Remember MF Global? That's exactly what happened there. Clients of MF Global lost all their holdings in those accounts. Even people who had no idea that MF Global existed lost assets. That's because the crooked company also served as a temporary conduit for assets passing from one place to another. This status allowed them to do some pretty funny things while they held those assets, often stretched out to a longer time than necessary. So when the company failed, those temporary assets went to a few derivative counterparty holders - JP Morgan prominently among them. JPM also functioned as the mediator in the settlement. The conflict of interest was legally blessed by regulators and the 'Morgue' walked away with a big chunk of the MF pie. Among those assets was a big pile of precious metals.

Easy money is a policy of low interest rates from the Fed combined with money printing. Banks can borrow quite readily. Initially, easy money leads to a boom in asset prices – wherever the hot money goes. In the 2000s, it was to real estate and its derivatives. After a time, the value is eroded by excess capacity of the assets – the system chokes on the flood. The values plummet – called the popping of the bubble.

Credit drives the global engines. New regulations (Basel III- from the BIS) are slowing down the use of credit. Well, probably good in a sense, but the ginormous global stock bubble is set to pop as well. That can only sustain itself if credit grows. The system must collapse in any event, but with the Bail-In set up at the 2014 Autum G-20 meeting, private funds are put on the chopping block. It may be deliberate controlled take-down of the economy - before it happens in an uncontrolled manner, but it protects the ultra-wealthy and jeopardizes the rest.

Few people know, but bank customers do not own their own deposited funds. The institution is the legal owner. You have only an IOU. Until recently, banks had to make good on the IOU with cash. That's changed under recent regulations. Now banks can require you to show a need for the money - and there are many reports of that happening. If the situation worsens, your deposit may suddenly become stock in the bank. This is not just idle theory or internet blah-blah. It's definite policy from FDIC and the Bank of England.

"Returning the sound operations of the G-SIFI to the private sector would be provided by exchanging or converting a sufficient amount of the unsecured debt from the original creditors of the failed company [the depositors] into equity." From there, the FDIC is off the hook. They do not cover your stock losses, only the loss from your cash accounts. Neat trick, huh?

Banks have been allowed, in court, to do anything they want with your deposited money. Every bank has become an investment bank. They can post your cash for collateral on anything else. If the bank goes up in smoke, the creditors can seize your money. They stand in line before you! Ask your financial advisor what he knows about this situation. If he scratches his head, then close your account fast.

In a Department of Justice announcement, large corporations cannot be prosecuted because of the potential damage to the economy. The DOJ is protecting criminals. And if they cannot be prosecuted, what will prevent them from stealing your money outright?

When the losses come from the debt write-down, massive wealth will be wiped out. Most bank monies will be vacuumed away in the rehypothecation settlement. Considering bank liabilities are many, many times bank assets - and these assets include your account and portfolio - everything could be put on the chopping block. And many things definitely will.

The flow of funds for Cyprus jags up suddenly, then back down for Eurozone banks just before the seizure in Cyprus. They knew what was coming, even when all other investors were in the dark. This gives two critical pieces of information for the investor. First, you will not be told directly what is happening. Second, somebody is manipulating this for big gain at the ordinary person's expense.

And remember MF Global? You probably head nothing about it after client funds were 'vaporized' (stolen). Well, the MF Global judgement is in - clients will receive some of their money back, if they agree that Corzine and JP Morgan have no criminal or civil liability. That's the system - if you rob people big and you are in the elite, you are not put in prison for world-record thefts. You get to keep most of the stolen money, but not all. Joe Biden appeared onstage with Jon Corzine not long before the theft. He proudly talked about calling him on the phone for economic advice. He was featured in political ads with Barack Obama. The system is rigged.

SoAsk your FA - are my investments subordinated to bank counter-party derivatives?

The Fed even released Bank of America "from all legal claims arising from losses in some mortgage backed securities the Fed received when the government bailed out the American International Group in 2008." The deal was secret, of course and only came out in 2013. It was reported by the NY Times. BoA paid a nominal fine, less than 1/10th of a cent per dollar of profit. Meantime, the Fed took the banks massive black hole obligations onto its balance sheet. And of course, the FED has no authority to abrogate the law in such a manner, but what does that matter? Some call it creeping fascism - defined as the merger of state and corporations.

The system is so over-leveraged that a mid-sized bank could cause a domino topple of a major bank, leading to a collapse of the system. Great wealth will disappear. It's only a matter of time until the next 'big one.' It will be bigger than the last.

Banks only hold 1% of customer deposits, even electronically. In a bank run, a few large customers can wipe out the cash holdings. Worse, the FDIC only has enough to backstop 0.3% of the system. The tiniest downdraft will wipe it out. It can't even float one good size bank. Most of the money is in bonds, loans, mortgages and other shaky investments. No one really knows what is actually on the asset sheet.

Federal Reserve makes it worse

The new head of the Federal Reserve is Janet Yellen. She's a dove - a monetary easer who thinks printing is a great idea. While it may be good for Wall Street and Washington - first in line at the trough - it's tough cookies for those with life-savings. That's people like you. Yellen thinks that printing will clear up the economy, get it back on track by priming the pump more. Trouble is - she totally failed to see the 2008 crisis. She told people not to worry. Wouldn't the Fed and the Obama administration have been a lot smarter to nominate someone who actually warned about the crisis? There are plenty of people out there.

There's also very good reason to doubt that further monetary expansion will help and some very sound reasons that it will cause further harm. Andrew Huszar, a former Federal Reserve official, directed the massive, trillion dollar plus MBS purchasing to bolster Fannie Mae. In the Wall Street Journal, Huszar apologized for further wrecking the US Economy. He stated that the Fed's printing to buy these instruments failed and left the economy near collapse. Quantitative Easing was run by him and it failed. Huszar noted that QE was actually a means to bail-out Wall Street from its notorious excesses. The Fed bought up lousy debt paper by the boatload; they did nothing to support the Main Street economy. They even actively blocked the dispersal of funds to the general economy.

This is financialization of the general economy. It punishes productive businesses and rewards speculative excess. It turns everything into a 'security' which can be sold and collateralized repeatedly, until the majority of the economy is an interconnected skein of credit and debt. Banks now have assets over 50% of the national economy. Since they need to constantly grow, this makes their effect on the general economy incredibly distorting. Because the finance industry controls such a huge share of the economy it takes the majority of any economic growth to sustain itself - remember the astronomical pay scales, for one thing.

This dynamic becomes horrendous when the economy is in contraction. The banks (and other corporate entities) are still trying to grow. In fact, because of the state of their balance sheets, they MUST grow or their horrible portfolios of junk paper will cause them to go insolvent - or rather make it glaringly obvious.

Huszar claims that the Fed is primarily a tool of Wall Street and it has sold out the country. This is the man who ran the program! For the Fed to buy such bonds ends a century of policy - the Fed was not supposed to directly intervene in markets - at all, ever. The Fed's policy was failing and Huszar pointed that out, but was ignored. No analysis of the benefits to cost ever occurred - despite this being the largest printing and spending operation in monetary history. Even government debt got no help. Huszar called it an 'absolute coup.' 2009 saw Wall Street make a killing while the general economy took a graceless swan dive. Things have not improved since then.

The total cost now tops $4 trillion. In spite of this, the economy has seen a paltry economic growth and even that may be doctored. The 1% bump amounts to less than $50 billion - a completely miserable loss of capital poured in by the Fed. The financial companies and the markets are now thoroughly dependent on Fed intervention and largesse. Because of its structural backstopping, monetary printing (QE) cannot be stopped. The Fed will jawbone and take it out of the public eye, but QE will continue in some form or other.

Due to this , the producer cost of goods has risen - and will continue to rise. This influx of capital to the finance centers generates speculation at an unprecedented scale - especially since they will not pay for losses, you and I will. Plus, the Fed gives inside information as to its activities.

Where does this leave you? In a more or less hopeless situation as an ordinary investor. You cannot win against these guys and the market is a zero-sum game. What does the average FA say about this? Nothing. He may express concerns about the excessive printing, but these concerns will stop at 'inflation' as the core problem. Believe me, your FA has NO IDEA at all of the real problems of the economy. He problems thinks it is merely a debt overhang that will never be repaid, but we will muddle through. Any thoughts to the contrary are 'doom and gloom.'

But the situation is potentially far worse. Continued printing and QE will distort the economy into so many bubbles and so much malinvestment that it cannot be unwound. No additional monetary printing will benefit. It will actually only aggravate the problem. This terminates in a crack-up boom - dotcom implosion extended to all aspects of the economy. If this overblown, please remember the demise of General Motors - supposedly one of the most staid, safe, blue-chip companies. And remember that the Powers that Be were threatening total collapse of the entire economy during the 2008 crisis. Maybe they were overstating the case, but maybe it's even worse now.

Growth is obsolete

The large-scale globalized project is hitting serious headwinds. Lack of cheap energy, debt creation to lunatic proportions, and centralized control leading to corruption, theft and crazy inefficiencies are just a part of the overall reality we are facing. The economy is in real contraction and the Central Banks are fighting it by printing money, trying to stimulate growth. But monetary growth is not economic growth. It's necessary to have good energy supplies that are inexpensive. Cheap energy is the real currency in today's economy. If the dollar fails, or the Euro, or any other currency (including gold), we can put in place another one. Currencies can be created in infinite supply. As long as people accept them as exchange for goods and services, they perform their function. We cannot run out of currency with no ability to find more because we create it.

Unfortunately, vehicles, manufacturing, air conditioning, stoves, and all our other conveniences do not run on money - they run on energy. Specifically, oil, gas, and coal - which is the base of electricity. Even solar panels are created using these 'stored' forms of energy. When the energy gets harder to extract, the economy will contract. It's called EROI - Energy Returned on Energy Invested.

In the heyday of the oil boom you could stick a straw in the ground in Texas or Saudi Arabia and have all the energy you ever wanted. Not so anymore. It once took 1 barrel of oil to liberate 100 barrels for the economy. That's the best EROI any society has ever enjoyed by a very, very wide margin. Historically 3-1 was great. Now the cheap oil is gone. Why else would they be spending so much effort on deep water drilling, tar sands, fracking, and shale oil projects. These have energy yields of 2-1 or less. When the entire scope is considered (full analysis is quite difficult), often they have a negative return. It takes 3 barrels of energy inputs to get 2 barrels to market. It doesn't take a PhD in economics to realize that no amount of money will make that work.

The global economy is in permanent contraction. The smart investor will realize that and invest accordingly. Mother Nature is about to force her point. We simply cannot find more oil. This is not an anti-drilling message. It is a pro-reality message. No matter how much we drill, the supplies are well-mapped out. All the super-giant have been found. There has not been a field over 20 billion barrels in 25 years.

The take-away from this seeming digression? The entire logic underlying the system is no longer valid. Your FA will continue to keep you in 'growth' investments. These are the Wal-mart, Merck, Exxon, and so forth stocks. These giant companies have no room to grow, especially in a contracting economy.

If I were to bet on any, it would be the energy stocks - oil supply is declining while demand is rising - their product will be worth more and more, but they will have to pay more to get it. However, the American companies are maxxed out. They are locked out of the best fields - those belong to Russia - now the world's number one oil producer. Ask your FA about investing in a Russian energy fund and watch him advise against it. You might also consider a Liberian oil company.

The important point here - the system is fatally flawed. It is headed for a series of increasing crises, or a major crisis that overwhelms the ability of the authorities to deal with it. Your financial adviser will tell you nothing of the sort. He will insist that the market is fine. Sure, there are imbalances and distortions and especially too much debt, but there is no fundamental problem. The markets will continue to function as they have always done.

He is wrong.

This financial system is coming apart at the most fundamental level. The international currency structure is undergoing the most significant change it has experienced in the past few centuries, possibly ever. The Fed and other central banks are trying to hold it together. The issues they claim are the problem are not the real problem. They claim it is... well, it's tough to say what they think is the real issue because Fed pronouncements are so garbled as to be meaningless. But it roughly looks like they want to goose the capital markets into sustainable growth and will use QE and bond buybacks and bailouts and whatever random dredge they can think up as an excuse to stuff cash into the big banks. The real thing they are doing is 1) keeping the banks on life-support and preventing them from lending money into the real economy (to limit inflation and serve their owners - the banks) and 2) transferring wealth from middle class to the very, very wealthy elites before the end of the current system. They will keep the game alive as long as possible to drain all they can before the big reset.

The real deeper problem is reliance on a fiat currency and use of that to buy votes and wage wars to hold onto the power of that currency on the global stage. It is an awesome power and it is easy to understand why they won't let it go. The imbalances from excessive printing of debt-based currency and hegemonic economic policies are caused by the central bankers. The rest of the world is tired of being subordinated to the Western banking cartel. The end is coming in the next few years. It is happening now.

Other nations will put an end however they can. Up to this point, they have not had the power - Russia was reeling from the collapse of the Soviet Union and China was effectively isolated by its own antediluvian policies and the might of US hegemony.

All that has changed. Russia and China have allied and brought numerous nations into their fold of economic trade. Many nations are beginning to pay for oil, metals and other goods in Yuan, Rubles and even gold. The total dominance of the US dollar is over. Other nations do not even need to force the issue - all they have to do is sit back and wait. They are accumulating hard assets to make the transition go in their favor, rather than devolve into chaos. They are forging alliances. They are trading dollar and Treasury reserves for land and resource deposits.

Your financial adviser will not tell you about this very real global dynamic, at least not in terms that will show you a threat to your portfolio. If asked, he will claim it is to protect you from making rash and stupid moves, putting your 'wealth' in danger by buying uncertain assets - commodities, precious metals and strong foreign companies. He is lying, or wrong. He has nothing to gain by your securing your portfolio in commodities. He will get no commissions by you investing directly in strong foreign companies, especially Asian or Russian ones. He is restricted from putting you in those investments. All he can do is recommend that you pursue them yourself. That would be in your interest. However, he will not do it because it is not in his interest. He makes no money.

Moreover, he doesn't even know. Your FA gets his market information, for the most part, from a company structure that treats clients as cows to be milked. He may in all innocence recommend that you remain invested solely in the domestic economy. But somewhere up that corporate chain, the management know what is coming. They are using their research teams to falsely validate keeping you in a failing domestic market.

How? Easy - they fire anyone that comes to a different conclusion. They feed them the results before the team does its research. Voila - the find what the management expected them to find - a strengthening US economy with the best bet to be investing in front-loaded mutual funds. Wow! I'm surprised.

This M.O. allows them to divest of their bad bets (yes, they have their own assets) by unloading them into your portfolio. This is what's happening. It is one of the many ways you are being sneak-attacked by the financial system. You are being used as prey by a corrupt structure.

End of the US Dollar's reign

Understanding Fiat

There's no argument—you have to worry about the excessive printing of money ~George Soros, Soros Fund Management

The banks, Federal Reserve and government will tell you that printing money is good - it primes the economy. It helps growth. What they won't say is that most of the money is staying with the banks. They are cycling it through their 'Reserves.' The Fed creates the money, loans it to the banks at 0.25% interest, then the banks deposit it at the Fed for 0.5% interest. It's a scam - free money for the banks that destabilized the global economy. And though a 0.25% bonus doesn't seem like a lot, when the amount borrowed is over a trillion, it adds up. This is how the banks keep cash flow from drying up. If it did, they would be unable to meet their obligations because they have made so much bad speculation. To put it plain, the major banks are in big, big trouble. All of them. The Fed loaned all the major banks a total of (make sure you're sitting) $26 trillion! That's Trillion. And the loans are zero interest. Of course, why pay back a zero interest loan? It's really a gift.

They did it to keep the banks from blowing up. And more than half the money went to European banks. Remember, this monetary creation is bad for the dollar - it devalues it. And your savings is probably measured almost exclusively in US dollars - also called Federal Reserve Notes.

Fiat means that state mandates the use of it. It does so by only accepting civil cases with contracts in US dollars. If you have a contract stipulated with gold payment, the court can't touch it.

Overall, this means that Federal Reserve (which is not really a government agency) can print as much money as they wish and they will not be stopped. And they have printed a LOT. The value of the dollar has declined by over 99% since the creation of the Federal Reserve in 1913. That means that your money cannot simply be saved - it will steadily lose value even as the numbers remain the same. That is called inflation, but it's cause is generally regarded as printing of money over and above increases in production.

And therein lies the rub. With this amount of debt overhang (our currency is created and sustained by and as debt), they must continue printing or the debt holocaust will be unprecedented. Your savings would be worth a lot more if they stopped printing. Every debtor would be scrambling for dollars, making them worth a lot more. But there are no restrictions on printing, so they are printing to sustain a flawed system. This drives down the value of the currency - inflation. But the amount of printing lately has been crazy. Price inflation has not even close to matched monetary inflation. But it will.

If the economy goes into reverse, then the dynamic is awful - further printing (more dollars) chasing a declining pool of goods. The Fed is controlling that by keeping the money behind bank firewalls. Hyperinflation will not commence from the domestic front. It will come from outside the country, if it happens. It will be foreigners dumping US bonds and cash in a panic. The value of the dollar will plummet on the Forex (world currency exchange) and prices will double overnight. It may not happen, but it is a real possibility. And our currency system has put that weapon, of our own money, into the hands of foreign, and increasingly hostile nations. The Chinese could easily cause a dollar panic by merely announcing the sale of all US based reserves. They may do so at some point - an act of financial warfare. It will only be when they are ready to roll out a global trade currency - not a reserve currency -

that would be many years later. When they have secretly divested enough US reserves in exchange for hard assets, they may well strike. Or they may not - it's hard to tell. But you can be sure they discuss it with the Russian government.

Your FA will tell you nothing of this. What will he say? 'China can't dump all their reserves - it would make their holdings lose value. Besides the US is their biggest market, they can't bite the hand that feeds them.'

This is hogwash. If China has enough gold (it does) then the sudden upshot in the value of gold would make up for all those currency losses. Anyway, what good is sitting on $3 trillion, if you can never spend it? For all practical purposes, their reserves are worth far less than the nominal value because of the distorting influence it would exert when they try to divest it. Do you think they want to get out of a system that pays them paper in exchange for enormous quantity of goods? Well, they are discussing it openly in university and on the streets. Finally, Europe is China's biggest market, not the US. They will try (are trying) to pry Europe away piecemeal, beginning with Germany. Russia is the proxy for this prying away.

Understanding this, would you want to be totally invested in the US market to pay your Financial Adviser's salary? Or would you rather position yourself for what is happening right now? Because when the lynchpin to the system breaks (it's already pretty cracked), the whole game begins to unwind. You get thrown under the bus. That lynchpin is the subject of the next section.

Petrodollar Standard

The Petrodollar Standard began in the early 1970's. After Nixon cut the dollar's last tie to gold, Kissinger created this stroke of genius. Beginning with Saudi Arabia, oil exporting nations agreed to only take US dollars in payment for oil. They then agreed to reinvest a large share of that money back into US debt by buying Treasuries. In exchange, the regime enjoyed the titanic support of the US military. That is why US military bases exist in Saudi Arabia. That has been the source of US power since the 70's. It has enabled the US to export massive inflation and run the largest debt of any country in all history. It relied on perpetual economic growth. If the dollar inflation outruns the global economic expansion, the dollar 'carry trade' on oil begins to unwind. The debt gets cashed in for US dollars, and the dollars get exchanged for finite commodities, precious metals and land. The US has maintained this standard for over 40 years, and the last decade has come with significant violence and war in oil-rich nations, like Iraq. This book is not about politics, but it is worth some thought as to why the US remains so vested in Middle Eastern affairs - is it only the 'terrorist threat', or are they defending something else, like oil?

I believe, with plenty of evidence laid out in my other book, they are defending the dollar's link to oil. Saddam Hussein announced an intention to sell oil for Euros not long before the invasion. Gaddafi was in process of launching a gold-backed currency and wanted to sell oil for gold when his ticket got punched.

That defense is failing. Russia is now selling oil to China for Yuan. Iran is selling oil to Russia for Rubles and gold. Other nations have begun to follow suit. No matter what you think of the dollar or US global politics, I urge you to put aside any nationalistic or other preconceived beliefs. This is not a moral question for the purposes of this book. I am just telling it like it is. The Petrodollar is about to fail, and with it, the dollar as reserve currency will also fail.

For certain reasons of trade and exports, etc. no single currency will replace it. It will be a consortium of the willing - namely, the BRICS - Brazil, Russia, India, China, and South Africa as leaders in their own regard. The key event will be Germany joining the Asian trade union officially. At that point, NATO will lose power. The Western alliance will disintegrate. Support for the dollar from Europe will cease - it is already in decline. Over the course of a year or two, the dollars will come home to the US. The dollar will suffer an enormous devaluation - 40% or much more. It might be up to 80%.

Think that through - your wealth, if it's in US dollars, will be cut in half or more. $1 million might only be worth $200,000. Many will be wiped out, unable to afford retirement. This may sound like some dark fantasy novel, but it is all too real. It is the consequences of abusing the privilege of the world's reserve currency by issuing too much debt and using it to fund the mega-banks big mistakes.

There is simply too much debt overhang - not just Treasury debt, but also corporate and personal debt. The choices are clear - allow a mass default and save the currency, but with an enormous deflation. Your money would become extremely valuable in such a scenario. You would become quite wealthy with only a moderate savings. However, they have proven they will take the other option - monetize the government debt and large chunks of the financial system debt. The Fed is printing money, lots of it in a separate channel like the Belgian Central Bank, to buy up the new debt issue. This is new money and increases the overall money supply.

Savvy investors and sovereign holders of US debt are watching. And they are acting. They are moving stealthily out of US debt. China is doing so very quietly. If China announced it was shoveling off US Treasuries, the debt market would collapse and the rest of their holdings would be worth nothing. The Fed is playing the game by purchasing most of the existing debt. That situation is temporary. Right now China is converting those paper assets to gold, viable companies, commercial real estate, and farmland - among other things.

That may be a bit long-winded, but I want to show you something no financial advisor will. You absolutely must take steps to understand this situation better and how to invest in it. You absolutely must take steps to protect yourself against what is coming. A dollar revaluation is mathematically inevitable. Most likely, it will be a devaluation - it will be worth less and probably a lot less. It will not disappear - not for many years, but it will move down the scale to a regional currency at best, possibly only a national currency. It is possible that many US citizens will repudiate if they find a viable alternative.

If you are long dollars, or hold dollar sensitive investments, you should take a long, hard look at this. See what means you have of protecting yourself. Develop a plan to downscale your US dollar exposure. If you don't feel competent, then get advice from someone you can trust who truly understands the situation.

Your FA will resist your attempts to extricate. He will imply you are a 'doom and gloomer.' Do yourself a favor - study the history of currency collapses. They are many. Thousands of currencies have failed versus less than a hundred that exist today. Protect yourself. Do it now.

Debt

During 2008, it came out that GSax was leveraged 333 to 1, JPMorgan at 52 to 1, and even so, they still wanted to do away with the fractional limit. That's why people who study it often refer to the fractional reserve requirement as a Ponzi scheme. A Ponzi scheme requires a growing pool of new investors to pay off the old ones. The need for new capital eventually goes parabolic. The bond complex of the US is the biggest Ponzi scheme in the history of the world. The need for new funds will soon overtake the ability of the Fed to monetize in any realistic manner, now that foreigners are dumping T-Bonds, adding to the stress. Hyperinflating the money supply will fail as the complex tears itself apart. More and more fixed income investments will be forced into the sucking maw as legalized measures push pensions and 401(k)s into the Treasury complex.

And that is the big point of warning. If you have a 401(k), you should look at divesting some of it, even if you pay a tax penalty. Argentina forced a similar retirement plan into government bonds, then essentially defaulted, leaving the public holding the bag. Banks with similar debt - the usual suspects - got paid for the bonds they owned. Again - they win, you lose.

The Fed bought 61% of all government debt in 2011. But it gets worse when the data is analyzed. Operation Twist was intended to flatten the yield curve. The yield curve is the yield rate of Treasury measured by bond duration – shorter term bonds tend to have lower interest rates. The 1 month T-Bills are hovering around 0%. People still buy them as a place to park big money, but keep it liquid. Operation Twist bought long-term (mostly 10 year T-Bonds) and sold short term (1 year or less) T-Bills. Obviously, selling short-term debt to buy long-term debt forces the institution to sell multiples of the buying. In other words, the purchased assets are on the books for 10 years, but the sold assets have to be rolled every single month – a rate of at least 10 times. And more short term assets are added each month, making the position more and more imbalanced.

The monetization also needs to perpetually increase because of the rising deficits and because legitimate buyers have left the building. At the same time, the tracks of it need to be hidden, but this is becoming more or less impossible. Only the public, which does not really pay attention to anything, can be deluded for long periods. Real investors cannot. Even the sleepy retirement and pension funds managers are waking up.

Operation Twist forces the timeline into an awful compression. As the huge Asian pools convert long-term securities to short-term securities, their average maturity gets shorter and shorter. This means that much more debt rolls over per month/year than previously. This compression will take a year to be created. When it unwinds, the effect may destroy the US currency and bond complexes. In other words, China, Japan, and other big US instrument holders can cash in all their debt – several trillion – in a year or so. At that time, the Fed will have to turn all the debt into dollars to roll it over. Existing investors don't want it – freshly created money will have to fill the bill. The defense mechanisms will be incredible to see. It appears that Operation Twist was designed for the Fed to purchase every 30 year bond ever issued. This is not a trivial matter – it is a cornerstone of the global monetary system. By monetizing it, global cheap money – the US kind – will begin moving very quickly. And quickly moving oceans are called tidal waves.

All this debt compels governments to devalue the currency and reduce its real value. Devaluation means more currency must be printed, of course, and that allows more debt to be repaid rather than defaulted. Of course, a devaluation also makes the holdings of savers worth less – unless they are very skillfully invested. Overseas investment has a lot of appeal when the dollar gets dropped. But it puts both governments and citizens in a tricky spot. Governments cannot announce a planned devaluation because all the money would leave the currency, sparking a massive psychological, then real, inflation – a devaluation before the devaluation. Usually, governments warn the well-connected elites, who can then preserve wealth (theirs, at least) and actually increase it. Ben Bernanke told a group of banking CEOs about the nationalization of Fannie Mae a few days early. They profited enormously from the illegal tip.

We have $9 Trillion in the bank, as a nation. Our total debt is $56 trillion. It's pretty easy to see there's a serious problem there. With debt at 6 times savings, something is totally out of whack. Of course, there is 'money' in the stock market, but not how people think. Once you buy a stock, you no longer have the money - the former stock owner has it. You have the 'value' of the stock, whatever the 'market' thinks that value is. I put these terms in quotes because in this evolution of a market, value is a very questionable idea. Since 99% of trading is on very short-term technical signals, fundamental value investing is essentially a monetary toilet.

What does your adviser say about this problem? What strategies is he using to protect your assets? Can you be sure they are not a sophisticated sleight of hand to protect company assets at your expense?

Inflation, deflation, disinflation, stagflation, and hyperinflation

When it becomes serious, you have to lie Claude Junker, President of the European Union.

The global economic situation cannot continue as it has. Something has to give. Major problems are on the horizon. The economic situation is presently so unbalanced that soon one of the 'flations will move out of control - inflation, deflation, hyperinflation, stagflation or biflation, all of them bad. This section explains those topics, how they come about, and how likely they are. Some will happen, at least nominally, for a time - others already are. Thus the important questions are the severity and the consequences.

First, a few words on the setup and why some dire occurrences are inevitable. Aside from the conditions already explained, the US fiscal situation is beyond any hope. The federal deficit is actually a mirage - things are much, much worse than the $1.1 trillion deficits typically put forth. The Treasury puts out the true government shortfall after the media numbers. They use Generally Accepted Accounting Principles, not the cooked numbers put out for the public.

The federal deficit was actually $1.3 trillion for 2012. But when the unfunded obligations are added in (shortfalls in Social Security and Medicare), the number is $5.3 trillion more. That was the additional amount needed for 2012 to fund future obligations - $6.6 trillion shortfall in total for a single year. It's 42% of national GDP, making the worst banana republics look like prudent savers. Total obligations are $85 trillion, over 5 times the officially advertised debt. Also, five times the official GDP. Remember: these are the official government numbers, not any third party ones. The government is telling everyone, in the open but without trumpets, that the fiscal situation is hopelessly insolvent. The media fail to report the real numbers. Even worse, the backstopping of the Pension Guarantee Fund, FHA and the Post Office are not included, nor are numerous bailout obligations for nationalized entities.

When a country hits GDP to obligations of over 100%, it's considered irreversible, headed for implosion. Only its world reserve currency status has allowed the US to continue faking it this far. GDP and taxation cannot possibly cover this, no matter the time frame. The government cannot squeeze additional revenue out of the private sector. The balance has been attained and maximized - increasing taxes will reduce revenues by damping economic activity.

At some point, soon, the government will be unable to meet these various obligations by taxing and borrowing. It is already monetizing significant amounts of debt through the Fed. Most of that activity is hidden and shuffled, but too many years of this and holders of US instruments get fatigue from falling returns and rising risk. There are no new investors and old ones want to divest. Printing money is the only option. Further mechanics of how this destroys the economy are covered in other sections. Here we simply look at how these forces play out against each other - deflation, the natural tendency of a fractional reserve system - versus inflation, the central bank's efforts to push it the other way. Quantitative Easing programs have steadily increased to the point where, at this writing, they are currently monetizing $85 billion per month of Treasury and bad mortgages. Monetization is inflation.

In situations of general economic deterioration, demand collapses, profits disappear, businesses fail and jobs vanish. Parabolic budget deficits in excess of $1 trillion require huge printing. Threats to the dollar from inflation can come from many potent macro-economic forces and situations which may loom in the future:

- Monetization. To protect mega-banks, the Federal Reserve is printing massive amounts of money, affecting the credibility of the currency.

- Economic systemic collapse. Another round of banking crises and failures would strain the budget and Treasury to the point of foreign abandonment.

- Failed Treasury auction. This would send a wake-up tremor throughout the bond world, bringing out global bond vigilantes - traders who force more honest interest valuations by speculating against manipulation - and causing nations to dump Treasuries.

- End of reserve currency status. If the world no longer needs dollars for oil or trade, the endless supply of dollars will have a far more difficult time finding a home.

There are virtually no positives for the dollar. Political instability, terrible trade gaps, inflation, government insolvency, financial systemic fissures, ultra-low interest rates and Quantitative Easing are all major dollar negative forces that are steadily worsening. Inflation is issue #1.

Inflation

By a continuing process of inflation, governments can confiscate, secretly and unobserved, an important part of the wealth of their citizens - John Maynard Keynes.

Inflation, every economist knows, is a tax. It is a hidden tax, because people do not lose money, per se - the money they have loses value by a process known as Seigniorage, wherein the issuer of a currency assigns it a much higher face value than the cost to produce it. The issuer gets the difference. By inflating the supply of money, the monetary issuer is able to acquire tangible goods and services in exchange for the cost of paper and the printing process. Not even that, when the process is digital. Loans under a fractional, fiat system are a form of seigniorage granted to banks. They are allowed to create money (thereby inflating the supply) and make their money by charging interest on that.

But the inflation tax, per se, is the value transferred from holders of cash (middle class) or credit (bond investors) to holders of value objects (gold, art, real estate) or debt (government and so forth). Governments can spend money at current value, before it inflates prices - since it causes that inflation. It thus gets new inflated money at value before that inflation hits and lowers existing (savers') money. Savers are effectively taxed by the loss of value in their holdings. If the government does it slowly, then the public never notices.

It's called the 'illusion of money,' and it fools people at an intuitive level. People measure in nominal terms - number of dollars - rather than purchasing power. All governments rely on this confusion in their citizenry. People do not comprehend inflation. If a hypothetical choice were posed to people - receive a 2% pay cut with no inflation or no pay cut and inflation is 4%- most would choose the latter, even though it meant they lost twice as much. People simply do not understand the real value of money.

Typically, a 5% annual inflation rate has been carefully managed (though control is now being lost). At this rate, returns to the creators of money and to the government are maximized without the public becoming upset. This means that a saver loses 5% of his income, leaving only 95% value at years end. This also applies to money saved from previous years. Any money left in cash for 50 years would be 95% diminished in value - this is the hidden tax that forces people to constantly seek returns on saved money instead of simply having enough for retirement.

Inflation is usually considered to be a monetary phenomenon. If more currency enters circulation without an increase in the supply of goods, then more money chases the same or fewer goods. Inflation is inescapable if more money is spent on the same amount of goods - it is mathematically definitive.

Looking back to the 12th Century, economic historian, David Hackett Fisher, found a recurring cycle to economic systems - a variable and volatile inflation with enormous wealth disparities culminating in total collapse.

Food and fuel led the upward movement. Manufactured goods and services lagged behind. These patterns indicated that the prime mover was excess aggregate demand, generated by an acceleration of population growth, or by rising living standards, or both. [1990s to mid 2000s]. Eventually, prices went higher, and became increasingly unstable. They began to surge and decline in movements of increasing volatility. Severe price-shocks were felt in commodity movements. [2008 oil price shock]. The money supply was alternately expanded and contracted. Financial markets became unstable. [2008 and after scenario]. Government spending grew faster than revenue, and public debt increased at a rapid rate. In every price-revolution, the strongest nation-states suffered severely from fiscal stresses.

All of this is happening, much as Fisher describes. Along these lines of increasing volatility, an alarming thing happened in June, 2012. The Shadow Banking system liabilities re-inverted, becoming smaller than conventional banking. The SBS liabilities first became larger than the traditional system's liabilities in 1995. Then in 2008, the liabilities reversed in the SBS and began to decline. In July, 2012, they crossed the line below the traditional system's liabilities. Why does it matter? It indicates that the SBS is undergoing a slow-motion debt deflation scenario - largely be getting out of that side of the business. That's why all the new money created - in the tens of trillions - has not entered the Main Street economy. The systemic liabilities have declined by $6 trillion from $21 to $15 trillion - a 30% drop with enormous numbers. The chart shows very clearly when the credit bubble popped. This is one big reason the economy will remain in recession. No new credit is being created. The SBS is deleveraging by market forces - the credit bubble is over.

According to the NY Fed, this is critical. The SBS functions as an inflation buffer. It performs all the traditional functions of credit transformation - liquidity, risk and maturity - but does so without any deposits. That lack of deposits prevents the shadow money it deploys from leaking into the general economy. It just drives up asset values and creates new debt-based assets. "The entire rickety shadow banking system is based simply on the good faith and credit that rehypothecated assets, converted into liabilities, and so on (think repos and reverse repos) courtesy of fractional reserve credit formation (recall rehypothecation), are valid and credible sources of liquidity." That functions in an expanding environment, but is a serious disaster in a contraction. As the SBS instruments mature and are cashed out, liquidity is taken out of the system since these credit instruments function as money in themselves.

The problem? The Fed has to create more and more 'flow' money to prevent systemic collapse. That money is rising in the conventional depositary system - which can leak into the general economy and quickly in a bank run. As the SBS continues to deleverage, the depositary base will rise. Within a few years, at current rates of movement, the depositary base will double from $10 to $20 trillion. And with it, monetary inflation. Price inflation follows.

Generally inflation relates to increases in the money supply more than to scarcity. If it comes about with an increase in population - more people need more money and they typically increase the supply of goods by increasing the work-force – it will not lead to inflation. However, central banks tend to create money at a far faster rate than population increases, as they favor facilitating opportunities for profit over stable monetary management, so we see a steady multi-decadal roll of inflation.

The velocity of money - how many times it changes hands - is an important factor in inflation. If people spend money faster, this increases the amount of money spent without actually increasing the money supply. In this book's argument, velocity is more a mass-psychology phenomenon, speeding up in relation to trust in currency, desire to get investment returns and to profligate consumer spending habits. Currently velocity is very low for a number of reasons but mostly due to the amount of new money that is parked in the reserves of banks that aren't lending. However, plenty of new money is leaking into the general sphere, largely due to massive government deficits. The expanding money supply is thus causing the current inflation, not velocity. Increased velocity, I argue later, is the main mechanism for hyperinflations.

Massive money printing (QE) results in a 'rising cost structure' without a compensatory increase in wages. The prices of commodities, durable goods, energy, and food all go up from speculative pressures but wages don't go up. People's income stagnates, dwindling in real terms. Industry suffers from plummeting consumption. Jobs vanish, incomes decline more. Pensions and savings cannot earn money in a zero interest environment. Savers and retirees have less disposable income. More money is printed to stimulate the economy, continuing the cycle of decline. Without an industrial base, an economy cannot grow. It can only burn up.

During inflations - currency and price - governments try to mask the results. They game the statistics. The US government is the reigning master at this ploy. Walter John Williams of shadow government statistics has been the chief unmasker of these ploys. The official Consumer Price Index (CPI) runs inflation at about 2% or so. However Williams, in 2013, claims inflation is knocking at 10%. He has solid data to show why. He merely uses the government's methods from 1980. There are quite a few inexplicable differences in these.

The CPI no longer measures the requirements to keep to a certain standard of living or increases to normal expenses. Deceptions are used to keep social security payments lower and to artificially inflate GDP to paint a false picture of economic recovery. This also makes real wages look better since nominal wages are deflated by the CPI to normalize them. A lower inflation rate produces less deflation on wages, so they seem stronger. But the truth of the situation emerges nonetheless in the fact that now most families need two workers to maintain their standard of living, while in 1970s, they only needed one.

CPI now measures 'core inflation.' This reversal of sense term means inflation excluding food and energy costs. The logic - food and energy are volatile and skew the 'long-run' rate of inflation numbers. This is ridiculous, of course. The long-run numbers would smooth out any volatility over time and any increases in food and energy would be properly incorporated into the data, and besides, ood and energy are the most critical consumer items. Along with shelter, they are the only true human requirements for physical existence. It is ludicrous to use any inflationary measure which ignores such essential items.

Inflation once measured a fixed basket of goods - some food, some gasoline, rent, and some non-essential items. There were no substitutions or changes in size or weighting within the index number. That changed in 1990. Politicians put forward the idea that substituting 'hamburger for steak' would result in a more accurate inflation measure. If people switched to hamburger, it was argued, they had merely substituted beef in one format for beef in another. Geometric weighting was also introduced, lowering the amount of any basket item that rose in price, on the assumption that people would then buy less. Accordingly, as far as CPI was concerned, instead of a 12 ounce steak going up 10% in price, it went down in size by 10%, keeping the inflation rate unchanged. It was lousy political cover for the change, but no one cared at the time. It only affected the cost of living adjustment for social security.

Weighting has become absurd. Health insurance is gaged at 4.3% inflation from 2008-12, even though all companies show rates going up by 25%. Even then, it's weighted as a tiny 1% of the basket, far below most people's expenses for health insurance.

Next came hedonics - downwardly adjusting inflation by a fuzzy measure of product improvements. If the price of vehicles went up 30%, then the addition of new gadgets (whether desired or not) were used to lower the inflation rate to meet targets. There may be some logic to it, but the price adjustments are non-quantifiable and arbitrary product changes are often marked as hedonic improvements to lower inflation numbers.

Inflation is further disguised by the dollar index. The dollar is measured against a basket of other currencies, but if all currencies are being depreciated simultaneously, there will be no decline in the relative measure of any particular one. However, in terms of real goods or gold, it will buy less. A true currency index would definitely factor in gold at 25% minimum.

One point is so critical, it deserves special mention. Inflation must be subtracted from GDP to get an accurate number for GDP. That's because if the nominal economy grows by 2%, but inflation is 5%, then all the purported growth and more simply reflects monetary increases. No productive increases or unit sale increases have occurred. In this scenario, the productive economy has contracted, not expanded. Leaving aside the issue of whether perpetual economic growth is good or even feasible, the question remains if it is in fact occurring. If the statistics are doctored downward by the government, then GDP growth is lower by the difference of true inflation to CPI. The numbers are clear. GDP is in steady, vigorous contraction.

Deflation

You cannot borrow your way out of debt - Daniel Hannan
Deflation is more or less the opposite of inflation. Money becomes more valuable. In a sense, deflation has happened in the computer industry for almost 20 years. Computers have become less and less expensive because of improved processing techniques, mechanization, in-built knowledge and economies of scale. This is essentially cost-push deflation - the manufacturers have made computers very inexpensive and made many of them. Measured in gold, we are in a true global deflation. Everything has been going down in value relative to gold for 12 years running.

Fear of deflation has become extreme. Portfolio insurance is at peak levels. Institutions are worried about debt defaults and money supply collapse. It's a difficult journey between inflation and deflation. The past few years saw $10 trillion in global money increases - the fastest rate in history in both absolute and percentage terms. The ECB has swollen its balance sheet to unbelievable levels; as of June, 2012 it hit 30% of European GDP. All of this is to fight deflation.

Former Fed chairman Ben Bernanke has openly asserted an anti-deflationary policy on any number of occasions. In 2002, he said,

sustained deflation can be highly destructive to a modern economy and should be strongly resisted. Fortunately, for the foreseeable future, the chances of a serious deflation in the United States appear remote indeed, in large part because of our economy's underlying strengths but also because of the determination of the Federal Reserve and other U.S. policymakers to act preemptively against deflationary pressures.

Preemptive action means printing money. Monetary expansion has a brief beneficial period during each iteration, but is subject to an extreme law of diminishing returns. After a few cycles, the process goes almost entirely negative. It does decrease volatility during the printing, Artemis Capital claims, but when the expansion stops, volatility goes crazy. High volatility is good only for very short-term traders. Long-term investors - the public, pension funds, etc - get crushed. In such a scenario, the best bet is to buy hard assets, commodities, and energy, and get out of the paper markets. Take the long view.

True deflation is what central banks fear - a more broad-scale currency contraction. At this point, people, businesses and governments become insolvent. They can no longer pay off the increasing debt-load. A burgeoning global default on the loans leads to banks being forced to write off a significant amount of bad debt. When a bank is paid off for a loan, the principal pops out of existence. The bank must nullify the principal. It is not allowed to create money and regard that asset (the loan) as still in existence when it is paid off. It can only keep the interest. They must do so whether the loan is paid or written off. In a deflation, everyone is looking for money to pay off debts. There's not enough of it, so money becomes extremely valuable. Prices decline because people hold on to money rather than buying things.

The main debate currently is whether the economy will run toward deflation or inflation - will the fractional reserve brute market force (deflation) overcome the unlimited monetary creation powers of the Fed (inflation)? As the chart shows, there have been no deflations since 1950 and no deep or sustained ones since 1930. But the conditions are far more extreme now, and analysts make the case that deflationary forces will strike quickly and overcome the CBs power to work against them. This seems unlikely, however, since Central Banks can create and dispense money in unlimited amounts in hours, and they definitely seem inclined to continue doing so.

In a deflationary spiral, businesses lose money due to lowering prices, then they fail. People lose their jobs and have less money to put into the economy, causing businesses to further lose revenue due to decreased sales. More businesses fail and the cycle continues. The cycle is horrendously amplified by massive debt. As prices fall, money becomes more valuable and people hoard it. The largest corporations and banks suck in all the money they can to survive - they are so badly leveraged that each drop in the debt markets (especially housing) causes seismic faults in their balance sheets and reserves. Because they are so large (more than half the economy) and so powerful, they dry up available currency in the general economy by not loaning it out again, once they have taken it in. This makes money needed to pay off debts, and just to survive, more expensive and harder to obtain, again exacerbating business failures.

Deflationists argue that Japan is a modern example of a deflation and that this fate awaits the US. Since 1990, prices in Japan have supposedly been in decline, causing economic havoc, because the banks have huge bad assets and won't lend. But it's not true - Japan has not experienced a sustained deflation. Prices have gone up and down, but on average, they are the same as in 1990. They've been flat. Japan has deflated for brief periods, but always seen a moderate inflation afterward to balance it.

In the US, according to Austrian theory, the 1930s saw a deflation - a money supply contraction - caused by 9000 banks failing. Depositors' funds vanished with them. The

125

FDIC was created in 1934 to make depositors whole and protect the banks from a run by eliminating the fear. Since then, the money supply has never again contracted.

The two causes of deflation of concern here are debt deflation and credit contraction. Debt deflation is described above. Credit contraction is when banks will not lend. In the current situation, bank balance sheets are so bad that they need to increase reserves defensively. Reserves are not loaned out because the fractional leverage is already very high from massive debt failures - they need reserves just to remain solvent as more debt goes bad. Moreover, in an ultra-low interest rate environment, there is lower profit but without diminished risk on loaned money, so banks have less incentive to lend. Instead, they have been given a risk-free 'carry trade' on US Treasuries. They can borrow enormous amounts from the Fed at 0.25% then reinvest in US Treasuries at 1-3%, or in Fed accounts at 0.5%.

Deflationists argue that the Fed cannot force banks to lend - it can only lend them money and hope. This is patently false, even absurd. Banks have enormous amounts on deposit at the Fed called excess reserves, on which the Fed pays a small interest. In fact, it's a scam in favor of the banks. This never occurred before the 2008 crisis, but now it is policy. Banks pay the Fed 0.25% for the money, then loan it back for a slightly higher interest rate. The banks are guaranteed risk-free profits for not lending. All they need to do is borrow enormous sums - and they have. To spur lending, all the Fed needs to do is charge the banks to keep the money in a Fed account rather than paying them for doing so. They can simply raise the rates until the banks have to start loaning in order to avoid losing money. Central bank activity is fighting debt deflation primarily by propping up the banks, then fighting inflation by preventing them from lending. But their activity does not lessen the credit contraction deflation, it worsens it. The Fed is lying about using QE to try to get the economy going again; that is only a ruse to give money to the banks while hanging Main Street out to dry. Routine deflation is not a real concern to central banks, because they can overrun it any time they want. The elephant in the deflationary room is shadow banking. This is the true deflationary threat.

This is where the Fed is banging its head on the floor. By QE, the Fed is reflating the conventional side of the system, where inflation is a short hop away, because of the need to expand the Main Street money supply through loans. Unfortunately, the shadow system is running scared. The Fed's monetary push is being used to deleverage the other side of the system. And the gap between shadow and conventional is growing. Analyst Tyler Durden showed that the gap shortfall since the Lehman collapse grew by $300 billion during the most aggressive part of QE. The Fed stepped up its fallacy with $85 billion in QE, going into the conventional system. For now, the inflationary genie is held in check by the shadow side's deleveraging. The big players know that the hugely controlled system currently in play cannot be sustained. They are getting out, unwinding the system piece by piece. Soon enough, the new money will seek a new home. With loss of faith in bonds, currencies, shadow liabilities, stocks and all sorts of paper, the managers will move the newly created money into hard assets - oil, gold, land, etc. When that happens, the next, and most destructive threat of all, will really come into play.

Hyperinflation

The surest way to overthrow an existing social order is to debauch the currency - Lenin

Hyperinflation is supposedly impossible in the developed world where money velocity is extremely low. But this ignores the emotional component of velocity that comes

127

into play very quickly when arising from fear.. The argument also ignores the weight of history. Strong economies have hyperinflated. Velocity is low in part because so many countries hold such enormous reserves. Japanese, Chinese and other large reserve portfolios take money out of the supply, in essence, but not out of their velocity calculations. If that money moves quick and public, other big money panics. Prior to the famous Weimar hyperinflation, Germany's currency base doubled with no corresponding inflation. Then suddenly hyperinflation took off. Prices rocketed by 20 billion times, doubling almost every 24 hours. Gold beat the hyperinflation at 1.8 times the average rate. Anyone who held gold saw their real net worth increase steadily. Everyone else was wiped out.

When the question of currency extinction arises, the knee-jerk response is that the US dollar is immune. Few know that the nation has already burned up two other currencies in hyperinflations, the Continental and the Greenback. One can add the Confederate dollar to the list. The average lifespan of a fiat currency is 40 years. The current Federal Reserve note turns that age in 2013.

The 'safe haven status' for the US dollar fell under serious threat with the increasingly desperate QE efforts from 2010 onwards. This marks the psychological beginning of the end for the buck. Panic selling of the dollar can happen without warning. The Fed and ECB will no doubt stand ready to defend it, buying dollars with other currency reserve stashes. This defense can continue for a very long time - traders are the ultimate setters of exchange rates and none wishes to cross swords with the central banks. However, a nation willing to take a large loss on dollar holdings could conceivably crash the dollar willfully. A concerted attack by Eastern nations would be devastating, though it is unlikely in the near term. They might even improve their situation by balancing these losses against a store of gold. Another trigger scenario is repudiation of the petrodollar standard by Saudi Arabia, though in the government's increasingly vulnerable position, this seems unlikely. The appearance of hyperinflation will be marked by a plunge in the dollar index and a rapid move to dispose of dollars and Treasuries.

According to fiscal and currency expert, Walter J. Williams, hyperinflation has been baked in since 2006 or so. Originally, he put the terminal date around 2018, but with Fed actions since the 2008 crisis, he has moved the outer limit for hyperinflation to 2014. His analysis is highly informed and detailed. The numbers are credible, based on analysis of government shenanigans. His prediction of hyperinflation, given ongoing Fed activity, is highly probable, but the timing may be off. A lot depends on foreign actions, especially those of China, Russia, and OPEC. At any rate, the government is trapped. It cannot work its way through the fiscal debt, impossible obligations and parabolic deficits without massive printing or direct default. There are no other options. No government given this choice has ever defaulted - it has always tried to print its way out, unwinding its debt via destruction of the currency.

Hyperinflation has different definitions. Cagan's is the most generally accepted: a monthly inflation rate over 50%. This is pretty staggering, becoming a 13,000% annualized rate. A $10 meal would cost $1300 at year's end. A far lower rate - 100% annually, doubling prices - would feel like hyperinflation to most people. In such a case, a gallon of gas would rise from $5 to $40 in three years. The International Accounting Standards Board cites several conditions in its definition, among them a 100% cumulative inflation over 3 years. In any case, in a hyperinflation, the rate of inflation continually increases and actually accelerates. As a country moves into hyperinflation, it might go from 15% to 35% in one year, then 50%, then 100%, then to a 1000%. At this point, the inflationary trend - the destruction of currency value - seems unstoppable.

It's widely agreed that at least 55 countries have experienced hyperinflation since 1900. t's a real threat. Hyperinflations frequently follow wars, severe crises, and deep social unrest. While they initially often stem from government engagement in foreign wars or need to service debt in the teeth of declining tax revenue, once hyperinflation has taken hold, it is exacerbated by government need to provide for the sheer survival of the people.

Some theorists consider hyperinflation to be merely a difference in degree of inflation. This is erroneous. Inflation is a monetary phenomenon - increasing ratio of currency to market items. Hyperinflation is a mass psychological phenomenon - repudiation of the currency. When the public knows the value will decline rapidly, they seek to fully divest of currency in exchange for objects of real value. In a slight inflation, people will hold onto large volumes of currency as legitimate savings. In a higher inflation (10-20%), people will instinctively feel that monetary savings are a losing proposition, but will not fully and instantly divest. They will invest in stocks, real estate and other instruments, then imagine their nominal increase is a real increase. They will still gage wealth in terms of the currency. In a hyperinflation, people panic and dump. Inflation is generally tied to supply of currency, and hyperinflation is tied to velocity of currency.

In hyperinflation, when people get paid, they immediately go to the store to buy things - they are dumping the money as fast as possible. Turnover of the currency goes up by hundreds of times. In severe cases, employees get paid twice a day. They rush away to spend the money on their lunch break. The process seldom continues for long. People cannot live this way - it's too anxiety-ridden. Their struggle for survival effectively becomes a repudiation of the currency, as they are forced to seek ways around losing out on their salaries' swiftly declining value. . An employer who can pay employees in a stable currency will become the employer of choice. .. A merchant who has a reliable barter system, alternative currency or a hard currency will instantly rise in prestige. Smart merchants are inclined to accept only precious metals, other stable currencies, barter, or direct labor for their goods. They will no longer accept the national paper. Governments typically respond with Draconian price controls and mandates to accept national notes. Shelves go bare instantly because of merchandise cannot profitably be sold at such prices. Stores operate at a loss until they fold because the money they receive is below operational costs. People resort to black market solutions. Supply chains are broken - no one wants to sell into a failing currency from outside. Producers with long wait times for payments go bankrupt.

All of this decimates real tax revenues, creating an ever-worsening fiscal problem. Unable to borrow or tax, the government prints money to cover its deficits. As the largest buyer in the economy, the government then pushes inflation ever higher. A destitute government can trigger hyperinflation in such a way. Tax revenues and investors become increasingly unavailable. The government must print the money to cover the unbelievable shortfall. The government then spends this money directly into the economy, driving up prices everywhere. An overwhelming feedback loop arises where the government must print more and more money to cover the inflationary death-spiral it has created. But this printing only causes prices to rise further. In the case of the US, the situation is exacerbated dramatically by huge entitlements, massive military spending, and enormous debt. The US government spent about $3.6 trillion on budget with a corresponding off-budget amount. That makes the government share of GDP over 30% without it having producing anything.

Virtually all models of hyperinflation blame excessive government borrowing and spending for it. Most models calculate a tipping point for government expenditures. There are many expenditures such as social security, medicare, pensions, military budgets and so forth that are not denominated in currency but set as target goals. When the combination of debt load, deficit spending, borrowing costs, and money printing accumulate to drive these costs up more than printing of money can accommodate, the government cannot improve its fiscal position. In other words, cost of operations will inevitably increase more than money created and spent because the government is driving inflation faster than it is increasing spending. Thus it falls further and further into hyperinflating deficit and debt. Simultaneously, it destroys the national wealth and standard of living. The next step is typically massive social unrest, followed by extreme changes in governance. Many credit Hitler's rise directly to the German Weimar hyperinflation.

It's important to realize that the actual supply of money in a hyperinflation does not increase nearly so much as the rate of inflation. There may only be an increase of 1000% in bank issued money, but the velocity increasing by the same will turn inflation into 1,000,000%. In the case of Zimbabwe, inflation became 22 quadrillion percent annually. Hungary experienced the highest inflation rate ever after WWII: 42 quadrillion percent monthly. Prices doubled every 15 hours. Governments simply cannot print the money fast enough to front-run inflation. As inflation reaches a critical tipping point - typically north of 50% annual inflation - velocity increases dramatically. In a stable economy, the money supply turns over 2-3 times a year. In a hyperinflation, the money supply can turn over 2-3 times each day.

There are about 120 currencies in use today. Over 600 have disappeared, 156 from hyperinflation. Of the others, most vanished from military take-over, phase-out into another currency, revaluation, or renaming. After these latter events, most currencies fail within 20 years.

It's useful to include a few lessons from past hyperinflations. The Weimar inflation is the most cited. After World War I, Germany had huge debts for war reparations. Initially, the country experienced deflation, which lasted for almost two years. Money velocity was low, the economy was performing, the currency was among the world's strongest. When it turned around, inflation was normal for a brief time, then hyperinflation struck with a vengeance. One person said it happened "like lightning...The shelves in the grocery stores were empty."

In 1791, France experienced a hyperinflation. Mobs raided Paris groceries. The state blamed merchants for the rising prices and imposed price controls. Trade halted. Food disappeared. High taxes rose further. Capital fled the country and the poor were abandoned. Price controls led to restrictions on sales of gold and silver, enforced by six years of imprisonment. Anyone taking the French assignat (the failing currency) at a discount could be fined heavily. In 1794, if someone asked which medium of exchange they preferred - paper or gold - before the sale, they could be put to death. The deteriorating situation ended in flames when the nation burned the assignats. In France's previous hyperinflation, John Law had made the use of gold and silver as currency illegal as well as ownership of gold itself. He closed the border to those leaving with PMs just before the fall of the French currency. Nations in desperate currency straits often clamp down on access to or holdings of precious metals.

The stock market is hitting new highs even as businesses fail from hemorrhaging losses and unemployment climbs the wall of worry. The coinciding of stock highs with a massive recession -depression even - is a clear sign of looming hyperinflation. There is another old warning signal of impending fiat failure. Most hyperinflations feature a disappearance of the coinage. As the metal in the coins begins to exceed the nominal value of the coin, their issuance ceases. Only paper notes continue to circulate. During the Roman hyperinflation, the coins were gradually debased by removing the silver content. The US has switched from copper to zinc for pennies. The metal in the nickel coin is worth seven cents (and is being removed). Smaller coinage is being taken out of circulation. It may seem less important, but when the penny disappears, mark that date down. Hyperinflation may be near.

Other 'flations

Fragility rises on long-term trend, with increasingly severe financial crises - Hyman Minsky

There are a few other 'flations. Though it sounds obtuse, the simplest is disinflation. This is merely a reduction in the inflation rate. If inflation ran at 10% in one month and 9% the next, there was a 1% disinflation. Disinflation is not deflation; it is still inflation, unless the disinflation exceeds the total inflation rate. Disinflation, if validly measured, indicates greater control over the inflation rate by the monetary creators.

Of more import is stagflation. In the 1970s, stagflation was the fear. Most people talked about it, but few understood it. In a sense, it's quite basic – rising prices, slowing economy with falling employment and lagging wages. Stagflation was thought impossible, until it happened. Rising prices were believed to spur production and hence job creation. More money creation was believed to be a panacea for a sluggish economy, and a consequent bout of inflation was a sensible price to pay. Economists were wrong - returns on printing declined quickly. It turns out to be more complicated. More money is just more paper. It is not more wealth and soon enough, the public understands this.

Stagflation is very intractable once it gains a hold. The tools for lowering unemployment contradict the tools for tightening inflation. Stagflation is politically measured by the so-called Misery Index: inflation plus unemployment.

It can arise from supply shocks in widely used essential goods, especially oil. When oil hit $150 in 2008, prices soared at the same time that economic activity contracted. Energy intensive businesses that were undercapitalized failed. Think of the auto makers. The key danger is a huge price rise for producers which cannot be easily passed on to consumers.

The second cause of stagflation is poor policy. If the Fed prints too much and the cost of labor is non-competitive (because the Chinese work for a lot less), then industry contracts while the money supply increases. Stagflation can also emanate from changes in the relative value of currencies, often from forex (currency exchange) markets, leading to severe price rises.

The above are more conventional ideas. The more hard money Austrian school finds stagflation to be solely caused by excess printing. Because the first ones to receive money (banks/financiers) benefit from it most by having increased purchasing power, and because those later in line (manufacturers/labor) are the true producers, money creation destroys productive capacity by weakening the producer's position in the capital chain.

In truth, the current economy will experience multiple phases, with some deflation, inflation, stagflation and possibly culminating in hyperinflation. Meantime, and from a more gold-based perspective, the current experience might more accurately be termed schizoflation. In some sense schizoflation, also called biflation, is always happening in real terms. As money moves from one sector to another, the sector losing funds experiences deflationary pressures and the sector gaining funds experiences inflationary pressures.

The current circumstance of debt saturation will create a predictable printing response. The increase in currency and debt will make biflation a powerful force. Necessary items - food, energy and so forth - are rising because of printing pressures. Big-ticket, debt-encumbered items are dropping because of lower purchasing power from recessionary and job loss conditions combined with unwillingness to take on more debt. It's a double hit for the middle class who still buy food and energy, and whose savings are mostly in paid off houses and bonds - debt-tied instruments that lose value. We will see meaningful deflation in debt encumbered assets (houses, cars, capital equipment, businesses), collectibles (baseball cards, old coins, postage stamps), paper assets (stocks, bonds, derivatives), and unnecessary items (left-handed potato peelers, chrome wheel rims, Christmas sweaters) and severe inflation in food, commodities, and precious metals. David Korowicz explains in more detail, by invoking the rising energy costs as lynchpin:

High oil prices feed back into the economy through reduced economic activity, increasing pressure on discretionary income and rising defaults. This is an accelerator of debt deflation dynamics. In discussing this we need to be clear about the definitions of inflation and deflation. Often, inflation and deflation are defined in terms of rising and falling prices. These are secondary effects. One can have rising prices in a deflationary environment. In this study, inflation and deflation are a rise or fall in money + credit relative to GDP [meaning - if printing outpaces production, that is inflation]. Debt deflation, even without rising food and energy prices, leads to reduced discretionary ... Rising food and energy prices, because they are at the heart of non-discretionary expenditure, lead to further squeezes on discretionary spending, credit issuance, and the ability to service debt. Thus economies are caught between vice-grips of debt deflation arising from credit over-expansion, and the rising costs of its primary needs. This reinforces a debt deflationary spiral.

Food is incredibly correlated to this cost because food production costs are almost entirely energy driven. As oil becomes more expensive and scarce, food will follow. As food is inelastic in demand, it will soak up more and more of people's money, drying up discretionary spending. This leads to civil unrest, beginning in poorer countries. Biflation is very punishing for a society and leads inevitably to social unrest.

Asset Confiscations

The welfare state ... always morphs into a system that provides excesses for the powerful few - Ron Paul

It's a well-known fact in some circles that desperate governments steal from their constituents. When they run out of money, they look for it in the closest places - citizen holdings. It goes back to ancient Rome - Brutus and his crew used 'proscription' to execute wealthy citizens and steal all their assets to fund an army. Henry VIII appropriated England's monasteries and took their wealth.

In the 1790's, the French took a great deal of Catholic wealth to fund the new government. During the US Civil War, the government took the property of people engaged in 'insurrection.' FDR later passed a law making gold ownership illegal. Then the Japanese-Americans lost their property and many their lives during WWII's interment. The Clinton administration 'borrowed' most of the funds in the social security trust to get a 'budget surplus.'

The above quote continues:

The insiders benefit during the bubble phase of the business cycle and are the first ones in line for the bailouts. The poor, for whom welfare is supposedly designed to help and for whom the politicians justify the spending, end up with the crumbs while the Wall Street/banking elites thrive in good times and bad. There are two problems. First is conceding the principle that government has the moral authority to redistribute wealth. Second is believing the redistribution will be managed wisely and without corruption.

After the 2008 crisis, Greece took money straight from bank accounts for tax evasion - with no due process of law. Cyprus seized almost 50% of bank accounts above $100,000. Spain forced its massive social security fund into government bonds. Europe has floated the idea of a 'supertax' on the wealthy - a one-time asset tax of 5-17% to cover the debt obligations of nations.

It will get worse as the situation grows more desperate. A huge part of the problem is the debt. There are not many options -

• let it take its course - deflation which will cause a wave of defaults and bank failures (ain't gonna happen).

• Inflation of the money supply to pay off the debts. in process, but the debt overhang simply grows with the inflation. Moreover, and maybe worse, it threatens the viability of currencies as people see their value erode. The high risk is full repudiation of a global currency like the Dollar or Euro.

- Take it from those who have it. Tax the wealthy. But don't worry - they won't hit the super-wealthy and the elite bankers. They will have ample warning and huge loopholes. It will only tap your rich Aunt Hetty.

Economic Collapse

You will see a system primed for a rerun of 2008, perhaps even faster and more intense this time ~Paul Singer, Elliot Management

The phrase 'economic collapse' is admittedly overused the days. What does it even mean? According to Investopedia:

An economic collapse is essentially a severe version of an economic depression, where an economy is in complete distress for months, years or possibly even decades. A total economic collapse is characterized by economic depression, civil unrest and highly increased poverty levels.

Well, the Department of Treasury ordered survival kits for all of its employees who oversee the federal banking system, according to a 2014 solicitation. Why? What do Treasury officials need survival kits for?

The emergency supplies would be for every employee at the Office of the Comptroller of the Currency (OCC), which conducts on-site reviews of banks throughout the country. The survival kit includes everything from water purification tablets to solar blankets. Survival kits will be delivered to every major bank in the United States including Bank of America, American Express Bank, BMO Financial Corp., Capitol One Financial Corporation, Citigroup, Inc., JPMorgan Chase & Company, and Wells Fargo. Items will also be delivered to OCC offices across the country, from Champaign, Ill. to Billings, Mont. The agency also has offices in Sioux City, Iowa; Joplin, Mo.; and Fargo, N.D. The mission of the OCC is to "ensure that national banks and federal savings associations operate in a safe and sound manner, provide fair access to financial services, treat customers fairly, and comply with applicable laws and regulations." The agency has roughly 3,814 employees, each of which would receive a survival kit. The staff includes "bank examiners" who provide "sustained supervision" of major banks in the United States.

"Examiners analyze loan and investment portfolios, funds management, capital, earnings, liquidity, sensitivity to market risk for all national banks and federal thrifts, and compliance with consumer banking laws for national banks and thrifts with less than $10 billion in assets," the OCC website explains. "They review internal controls, internal and external audit, and compliance with law. They also evaluate management's ability to identify and control risk."

Not the profile of a high-risk job, needing this sort of thing. What are they worried about? Maybe it's just more government nonsense, but maybe they know the economic collapse, complete with rioting and shutdowns, is already baked into the cake.

Pensions and retirement accounts

Another sign of severe economic stress is the pension crisis. It may seem like a small part of the puzzle, but pensions hold a huge amount of cash...and 'debt.' They cannot cover what they need to cover. So they are covering it up. They're taking the liabilities 'off-balance sheet.' This used to be a criminal act, but the laws are easier now. If a company has a huge financial hole, it just takes it off-balance sheet to prevent a hit to the stock price. Verizon and GM both shoved off a total of $32 billion to Prudential insurance.

But it's just as bad for the government as the private sector. The gov can raise taxes (won't fly) cut entitlements like Social Security (and lose an election?! just to save the country?) - not gonna happen, print it (partially happening, but would put too much stress on the already stressed machinery to monetize it completely), or steal it from private pensions. They are doing this slowly, by essentially forcing the pensions to invest in bad Treasury paper. The people will not have a veto.

Even more, the ultra-low interest rates have crushed pension funds. Managers cannot make enough returns on the funds to pay the pensions out because Treasuries (the bulk of their holdings) only pay about 2%. That's below inflation! They are losing real value. To add insult to injury, they must add huge amounts of capital to the base fund in order to get the amount of returns needed to just pay the pensions. But that capital comes out of reserves, intended to backstop the company or grow the company. Those reserves represent a drawdown, hitting the company's productivity, bottom line, and eventually, the stock price. But for most people, it really means that pensions are dead. And existing pensioners? You might get another 3-5 years, but then your pension will be insolvent. It may pay some trivial amount, but inflation will have long destroyed the value. What good is $2000 a month when a loaf of bread is $100?

Most pension funds are dramatically underfunded and malinvested. Municipal funds are blowing up right and left - Detroit is finished and most workers retiring today from the city will not see much retirement income at all. The entire state of Illinois looks likely to default on pension obligations. GM needed a bailout largely because of its generous pension fund. Many of these funds will be gone in a few years if they aren't already. And many people will not find at the end of their work rainbow a pot of tin and government bonds.

A large part of the problem is the wrong-headed projections about possible returns to pensions. Some of these are over 8%. In an era when risk-free rate of return is about 2%, that's not realistic for a large, highly conservative pension fund. The managers are getting desperate. While equities have helped that by going steadily up, bonds have performed awfully - signs of a Fed goosing the market by issuing cheap money in a 'virtuous circle' with the banks. But equities are ripe for a serious correction. It remains to be seen how long the levitation can last. When the correction comes, pension funds are going to lose money. Then the emperor will be fully revealed naked. Cities and states apportioning unrealistic percentages of the budget to pensions will suddenly find themselves deeply underwater. The only way to get air will be - cutting pensions dramatically. And guess who runs most pensions? Money managers - specialized financial analysts.

Retirement accounts represent another bugaboo. It's similar to the Mutual Fund account described earlier. Fees amount to 1% - but that's the cost from the entire balance, not from profit. It doesn't matter if your $100k retirement account goes up or down that year - the fund gets $1000. Next year, another $1000. And next year, the same. If they lose you 50% of the value, you still get tapped for $1000 because they are usually Class C funds. You pay at the beginning of the year, not the end. And that happens every year.

One investor rode the Dow 12% gains in a private account for, well, 12% gains. His retirement account, in essentially the same stocks, lost money. This was in a stellar year for stocks. Why? Multiple fees. Not only are there management fees, but also sales fees. These can account for up to 8% of the difference between what you pay and the Net Asset Value. The guy who sells it usually gets over 5%, even if you send the order in directly. He does nothing, but gets a good chunk of your savings. Other hidden costs can triple the amount you pay for your retirement fund.

In the end, a $100k fund with normal asset valuations for 50 years might be worth $240k at retirement. Adjusting for inflation, that's actually less than is put in. And the financial institution gets the same amount as you did - $120k of cream, only it is profit for them. They didn't put any money in, so they don't get hit by inflation. It's all profit.

The system exists to bleed you to death. Literally, until you die. And beyond, but we won't get into the inheritance issues faced by the lower tiers of wealth. It's not an accident, either. The whole thing was designed that way.

Recommendations

Currently, there are more and more people recognizing that the 'gold is useless' story contains too many lies. Gold now suffers from a 'smokescreen' designed by the US . . . to maintain the US Dollar hegemony ~ Sun Zhaoxue, Former President of the China Gold Association

Friends don't let friends buy stocks. Okay, I'm joking, but for the quick reason - look at this chart. P/E means price to earnings ratio. That's the amount of total capital worth for all existing stock (price X shares) divided by the amount of money made in one year. Average valuations are around 14.5 long-term. A dip below 10 (meaning 10 years to earn back all existing equity) is considered a screaming buy. Above 15, a clear sell. As the chart shows, companies are at high P/E ratios. At 20 years to earn out all equity, the average corporation is mortally ill. They don't need Federal

Reserve medical treatments - they need a priest. It looks like it's coming down since 2000, but I believe (with evidence) that much of the decline in ratio is due to 1) crooked accounting and 2) stock buybacks based on selling bonds (swapping one debt for another).

It's better than 2009 when ratios briefly tapped out at 123, but these are companies that will be issuing more and more debt (stock, bonds, or whatever) just to survive. Stock issuance waters down previous stock, making it less valuable and large bond issuance spooks the bond markets, driving up interest rates and putting massive strain on profits. P/E ratios only worsen, except when the stock price tanks. When it does, the sheep get fleeced. Nobody wants to be a sheep. If you insist on buying stock (and owning some is not bad), here are the best rules I know.

• Blue chips are dead - they were never a great buy for the average investor. They're good for the Warren Buffets who push massive amounts of capital around and need very liquid markets, but they're pretty low-profit for the masses. The Buffets get sweetheart deals for sinking huge capital into the chips.

• Look for the lowest P/E ratio you can find. Look for well-capitalized entities. Make sure their accounting procedures are GAAP-based. Financial entities have 'national security exceptions' to Generally Accepted Accounting Principles - they're allowed to write fictitious asset values because they're considered so important to the economy. In short, their balance sheets are garbage.

• Stay clear of businesses that are at the end of a bubble phase. Be leery of AAPL and GOOG - these are great companies, but it's hard to tell when they're going to top. AMZN is a danger spot - it performs very well, but Amazon has made a profit in only one quarter! They have excellent cash flow, enormous lines of credit and untapped bond potential, however, so that keeps them 'up.'

- Remember, the Facebook IPO crushed the suckers who bought in early. The market for hot stocks is overbought. Don't listen to internet blather about the next secret moonshot stock, either. There are a lot of pump-n-dump operations out there. They buy a small stock, talk it up till it moves from investor interest, then dump their shares at a profit. (I got caught by this early on and will not again.)

- Fake accounting standards make it impossible to tell a solvent company from an insolvent one. A company may look great on its balance sheet, but it's now (more or less) legal (for a lot of companies) to simply move any liabilities off-balance sheet! They could owe a trillion dollars, but legally omit that in quarterly and year end reports.

- Learn the options security technique called a straddle. It's a defensive technique to prevent steep losses - and it's free.

- Learn about the real rate of inflation - published by shadowstats. You must beat this rate or you are losing value. Very few investors understand this, or the power of the 'inflation tax.'

- Regression to the mean is among the most critical medium term investing concepts, yet it is totally lost on almost all financial analysts. If a stock exceeds its historical performance for a time period, it will almost inevitably return to its former trendline. Using this simple tool, you will save tens of thousands or more over the lifetime of your investing - just by waiting until the right time to buy/sell. Your FA will likely never do this.

- Learn how to direct register your stocks. It's not that hard and it makes sense for any buy and hold stock.

Here are the pros and cons of direct registration. Counterparty risk is drastically diminished. Sure the company can ruin its balance sheet and kill the stock price, but if your brokerage rolls over, your stocks may be given away to make good on their debt. Your stocks are used as collateral, remember? With DRS no one can pledge your stocks as their collateral.

You also get material straight from the company - it gets their faster. Often, going through the brokerage, you will hear about annual and quarterly meetings after they have taken place. The DRS does not use paper certificates. If your house is robbed or burns, you still own the stock online.

DRS stocks cannot be sold short. Did you know that all of the shares you own are short-sellable through your brokerage? They can loan them out to other clients, who then sell them on the open market. This drives the price down! Your stocks are being rented out (there is a small fee) to help lose you money.

You don't pay brokerage fees to get in. If your broker buys the shares for you, you often pay 2% or so. That means your $10,000 purchase only nets you $9800 of stock. You started out with a 2% loss. Go direct and get a full $10,000.

With DRS, you can use the DRIP (dividend reinvestmen program) to easily accumulate more stock.

Transfers to other people (family, etc.) is very easy. This can help with a gift to children up to the gift tax exclusion limit every year. This will save your legacy a great deal of tax hit when the estate is settled. The stocks have already been transferred - tax free!

The main downside is the lack of liquidity - it takes a few days to post your stocks for sale. That can be a big negative in a large sell-off, but it can be countered with a disciplined program of using collars. You can have your shares in a brokerage account, but still direct registered. Ask the transfer agent and he will take care of it.

You may want DRS for large holdings you intend to keep for a long time. Especially if you're concerned about weakness at your brokerage or some of the less palatable activities like rehypothecation or loaning to sell short.

If you are in need of a financial adviser, I highly recommend a fee-only adviser. This represents no conflict of interest. The adviser makes the money in a straightforward manner. His interest is aligned with yours - if he makes you money, you will recommend his service. If he loses you money, you will not. The conflicts of interest inherent in the traditional industry will eat your portfolio alive- it has happened to many people. Most people who have gone to this industry for help. It may be impossible to find a competitive, risk-balanced return from the financial services industry. Clearly, mutual funds fail miserably.

Some tactics to consider:

• Buy calls on SPY at the right time. Since the Fed is supporting the market, whenever there is a crash, it climbs right back, very quickly. If you had bought $190 OTM calls for a 2-week expiration right after the November, 2014 market crash, every dollar invested would have turned into $16.

• Sell a bear put spread right after a crash. The cost of options is highest when volatility is high, so selling a put spread a few dollars below the market level will net a good payout. If you sell it for a long-dated expiration, you will get a large percentage of the spread amount. When the SPY rises, the cost of the spread will drop quickly for 2 reasons - volatility costs will collapse and the spread further out of the money. You can close the trade out quite quickly for a strong profit. There is risk, of course, if the crash goes further down. But the long-dated expiration serves a second purpose, allowing you to wait for a market recovery.

• Sell naked puts weekly on steady rising stocks. Most people think naked puts are horribly dangerous and prefer the seeming safety of covered calls. Here's something few people seem to know - covered calls and naked puts have exactly the same risk/reward profile. Naked puts tie up a lot less capital, however. The proof is bit complex for this book but interested parties can contact me directly for that explanation. An investor who sold Google puts for the past several years would have seen their 'money at risk' more than double every year. The downside is the outsized hit your portfolio will occasionally take.

The final recommendation, at the risk of sounding like a crank, is to buy physical gold and silver. If you have time to read Gold Wars: the Battle for the Global Economy it goes into the arguments much deeper. The book also lays out the long-term suppression of the precious metals market and the reasons for this. I believe that all capital markets are manipulated. To some extent this is inevitable, but the current realities are extreme. That's because the manipulation is a collusive effort among the most powerful players in the capital markets - the Central banks and the West's largest banks. All the major banks and investment houses are participating and, believe it or not, all the high-level actors know the game. They don't want to blow the whistle because they are getting huge rewards for doing their part. Meanwhile, you are paying the price.

You may think you're doing okay, if the markets are still rising when you read this. But there's no telling when the crash comes. The fundamentals are so distorted that the unwind will be epic - like nothing ever seen. This extreme of manipulation has never been enacted on such a scale before. When it was attempted on much smaller scales, the result was always the same - it worked for a while and the sectors manipulated exploded - until they crashed. The smart money walked away whistling and the dumb money jumped out the window. You're not the smart money and you never will be - that club is restricted. But that doesn't make you the dumb money. The question is - even if your portfolio is temporarily up, what is your downside protection? Grill your FA on this, and if you don't like the answers, terminate the relationship.

The suppressive tactics on precious metals is a bit new. Short selling and capping markets has not been so lucrative until recent innovations in market auction structures have opened new doors of possibilities for the institutional pockets. According to many market analysts, such manipulation cannot last forever. This is true, but how can long can it last? Most analysts believe the powers cannot fight the market - it is too powerful. I'm not sure I agree. I really don't know how long they can maintain the suppression. It could be a long time. However, other sovereigns are demanding physical gold in massive quantities. They are draining the Western supplies at fire sale prices. At some point, they will be ready for the price to rise. And rise it will and deep and strong and steady for a long time. The first phase will be a sharp upward revaluation - probably a doubling for gold and a tripling for silver. That will begin the next great bull market in precious metals.

From that point, metals will rise steadily for many years. To assist it, the BRICS nations will roll out a gold trade settlement product, perhaps a gold-backed currency or a group of them. No nation will, or can, do this alone. They would be victimized by their own success and any export market would go up in smoke. This is because their currency would rise so swiftly that their exports would become incredibly expensive - too expensive for most people to buy. This complicated topic is beyond the scope of this book, but the result is that some form of gold backed exchange note will be coming in the not too distant future - by 2020 at the latest. Probably sooner.

When that happens, holders of gold will become much wealthier. Holders of silver will see even that gain magnified by quite a bit - probably twice or more the gains in gold. My recommendation? Buy some physical precious metals. Do not buy GLD or SLV - buy physical, allocated gold if you feel comfortable holding it in a secure location you trust. Market instruments for this are CEF (an allocated, audited fund with both metals), PHYS (allocated, audited gold), and PSLV (allocated, audited silver). There are other suitable instruments - notably SLW (a silver royalty streaming company) and FNV (a gold royalty streaming company. Most in the know, slower moving investors are 30% metals - at a minimum. Some are up to 100%.

For the more sophisticated trader, you might consider the 'ultimate hedge.' This is to short paper gold and go long physical gold. Let me break this down - paper gold will never cost more than physical gold - except for brief aberrations and there are pretty powerful market limits to how far this inversion can go. Right now, CEF (a fund with real gold and silver) is selling at about a 5% discount to spot gold. This can continue for a while, but it's unlikely to get much worse. And it should correct itself. When gold rises, it definitely will.

The technique then, is to short a paper instrument - gold futures or GLD, probably. Then go long CEF in the same dollar amount. As long as the relative prices remain, you will neither make nor lose money when gold rises or falls. A loss in the phys will be answered by a corresponding gain in the paper and vice versa.

At some point, many believe, the game of shorting huge amounts of paper gold will end. At that point, physical will sell for a 'premium,' as it did after the 2008 crisis. Silver in shops was 50% higher than the spot price of silver. When the rig ends, the paper price of metals will drop or flounder sideways. The physical price will shoot up dramatically. The two instruments will separate. You will make money off the rise in physical. The paper you shorted will protect you from any takedowns in the meantime. This may take a while to realize and it may not ever happen - nothing is sure in financial markets. But it represents a very strong opportunity to profit from extreme market distortion, with almost zero risk. That's a rare thing.

And you know what? I think the major banks are positioning themselves in precisely this way right now.

Thanks for reading

I hope you found Invested to be Molested useful. It took a lot of research and many, many hours of writing. I want it to save people from a pretty bad system. Hopefully, it will protect people from the current state of affairs.

If you found this information useful, please review the book at your retailer. Your review really counts in multiple ways. First, it helps me to improve the book. Let me know what you think. Let me know what you'd like to see in the next book! Also, it helps the book get noticed by the Amzn algos so people know it's there. As a writer, this is critical. It's how we survive. It also helps out other readers to know when they've found a good book.

So, if you have a few minutes, I'd really appreciate it if you clicked over to the review page on Amazon and let the world know what you think.

I am available for reader questions, input, complaints, or chats at misterkel@gmail.com.

Thanks for taking the time to read Invested to be Molested. I genuinely hope it protects you from financial predators in sharkskin suits.

yours,

Kelly Mitchell

About the Author

I am a small-scale private investment advisor and a writer. I charge on a fee-based scale, depending on time needed. My rates are variable, but very reasonable in the industry. I have been an investor and trader for 15 years. If you're concerned about some of the issues in this book, contact me.

I assist clients by giving specific reccomendations based in large part on the advice in this book. I specialize in option spreads and precious metals. Clients typically need $100k or more to make my service useful. Interested parties can email me at misterkel@gmail.com.

Limitation of Liability

The author assumes no liability for any information or action based thereon by the reader in any context.

Table of References

Zagor6, Reddit.com/financial_advisors

Judicial Apartheid: Wall Street's Kangaroo Courts (Part I), Pam Martens: July 20, 2009.

5 questions that will change your future, fool.com, 2013.

Silver Update 80812 - Busted Trust. Brother John F. Youtube.

Hypothecation. Wikipedia.

The (sizable) Role of Rehypothecation in the Shadow Banking System. Manmohan Singh and James Aitken. IMF working paper 1072. 7/2010.

The Real Bombshell in the MF Global postmortem. Yves Smith, Naked Capitalism, 6/5/12.

BCM has ceased operations. Ann Barnhardt, Barnhardt Capital Management. 11/17/11.

MF Global Lawsuit puts Pressure on JP Morgan: Bullish signs for silver as Comex rehypothecation exposed. Silver Vigilante. June 5, 2012.

Exposure of Banker Corruption. Jim Willie, July 5, 2012.

MF Global's U.K. Administrator KPMG Says It Knows Where Clients' Money Is. Kit Chellel. Bloomberg. 12/16/11.

Let's Make the Clawback Risk Real. Karl Denninger, Market Ticker. 12/6/11.

CME Group letter, July 23, 2012. Terry Duffy and Phupinder Gill.

US markets liquid and deep or rigged and broken?, Martens, Pam and Russ. Wall Street on Parade, Aug. 26, 2014.

did-psychopaths-take-over-wall-street-asylum-commentary-by-william-cohan, Jan.2, 2012.

why-dont-the-psychopaths-on-wall-street-and-in-d-c-show-remorse-for-their-destructive-actions-and-why-dont-we-stop-them, Washington's Blog, 7/12.

Section from Gold Wars: Battle for the Global Economy, Mitchell, 2012.

Shadowstats.com

No. 445: SPECIAL COMMENTARY - Review of Economic, Systemic-Solvency, Inflation, U.S. Dollar and Gold Circumstances. Walter Jon Williams, Shadow Government Statistics. June 12th, 2012

Shadow Banking. Federal Reserve Bank of NY staff report #458. Zohan Pozar, et al. 2/2012 revision.

Hyperinflation Special Report 2012. Walter J. Williams, Shadowstats.

Benjamin Bernanke, Federal Reserve Board meeting, Nov. 21, 2002.

The Fed Has Another $3.9 Trillion In QE To Go (At Least), Tyler Durden, ZeroHedge.com 9/23/2012.

Williams, Hyperinflation special report 2012.

History of Fiat and Paper Money Failures: The Fate of Paper Money. Mike Hewitt. rapidtrends.com.

2012 Hyperinflation report. W.J. Williams, Shadow government statistics. Jan. 25, 2012.

Trade-off, David Korowicz. June, 2012.

They're Coming For Your Savings, John Rubino, October 12, 2013.

Elizabeth Harrington, 12/10/14. Free Beacon.

www.ingramcontent.com/pod-product-compliance
Lightning Source LLC
Chambersburg PA
CBHW070858180526
45168CB00005B/1867